'More often seen as a sourc  overlooked as a potential re: macy. The 2019 Abu Dhabi signed by Pope Francis and a new international dialogue common human desire for peace. This fascinating book plunges deep into that dialogue and gives us hope for a future where the engagement between religions, global politics, and human rights can push us into a new and more reassuring era.'

—Mary McAleese, Former President of Ireland

'In this moment of fractured politics and dissolving ethics, renewed attention to religion as a source of unity is a bold and much-needed initiative. The tradition is long and the ideas are inspiring. This volume provides a practical guide to creating a new dialogue suited to the distinct challenges of the 21st century.'

—Joel H. Rosenthal, President, Carnegie Council for Ethics in International Affairs

'I warmly recommend this original book to all those interested in the values underpinning multilateral diplomacy. Today's challenges are set out clearly – epochal changes in the natural world, the virtual world, and in politics. The authors put forward "axioms of the historical imagination" with a view to an inclusive, values-led, fit-for-purpose global diplomacy over the coming decades. At a practical level, they propose guidelines for innovative processes under UN auspices – long-term, regional, and multi-layered. They argue persuasively that well-judged forms of engagement between public authorities and religion (and other "life stances") can contribute meaningfully to sustainable development and to the changes in habits, assumptions, and actions that are urgently needed at a global level.'

—Michael Møller, Former Under Secretary General of the United Nations

'Finally! Diplomats call other diplomats to take religious and cultural values seriously as irreplaceable subjects of foreign policy planning and peacekeeping doctrine. Centres of academic research have offered compelling evidence that tradition-based values motivate tendencies to both violence and peace in conflicts around the globe and that successful peacekeeping must acquire capacities to address such tendencies. But this time, the argument comes from the diplomats and practitioners themselves. In this compelling and urgently needed book, distinguished ambassadors and peacebuilders argue that the international community has lost its consensus on the values and beliefs that would enable it to respond effectively to today's unprecedented challenges to human civilisation. It is time to re-explore the world's deepest wisdoms from East and West, North and South, to regather ideals that drive human desires for peace, and to reinvest those wisdoms and ideals in global institutions that effectively serve humanity's most pressing needs. But how to reinvest? What gives me greatest hope are the authors' practical recommendations: detailed analyses of how agencies like the UN, OSCE, and the EU can expand institutional doctrines and strategic plans in service to this multi-civilizational vision of human values. Here is reason to hope that there is still time.'

Peter Ochs, Edgar Bronfman Professor, Department of Religious Studies, University of Virginia

ON THE SIGNIFICANCE OF RELIGION FOR GLOBAL DIPLOMACY

What could it mean, in terms of strengthening multilateral diplomacy, if the UN, the Organisation for Security and Cooperation in Europe (OSCE), the European Union, and other regional diplomatic frameworks engaged more creatively with a religious perspective?

In this ground-breaking volume it is argued that international organisations, backed by governments, can and should use their convening power to initiate new, multi-layered *frameworks of engagement*, inclusive of the representatives of religion. This can make multi-lateralism more fit for purpose and have a major impact over time on our planetary future.

The book is divided into an introduction and six chapters:

- Towards a culture of encounter inclusive of the world's religious traditions
- Structural questions in 21st-century diplomacy
- Knowing what we ought to know: the issues that face 21st-century diplomacy
- Towards the global objective of a common peace for humanity
- Understanding how change happens
- The diplomacy of the two standards
- The development of new frameworks of engagement

A brief outline is offered of what an all-European initiative – an *agora for Europe* – might look like if, in the 2020s, there were the political will to inaugurate a European regional process reflecting the orientation and methodology proposed in the book.

Combining cutting-edge research and reflection, with concrete recommendations for academics, religious actors, policy makers, and practitioners, this concise and accessible volume helps to build bridges between these oftentimes separated spheres of engagement.

Philip McDonagh, a former ambassador, is Adjunct Professor and Director of the Centre for Religion, Human Values, and International Relations at Dublin City University, Ireland, and Distinguished Global Fellow at the Center of Theological Inquiry, Princeton, USA.

Kishan Manocha is Head of the Tolerance and Non-Discrimination Department at the OSCE Office for Democratic Institutions and Human Rights in Warsaw, Poland.

John Neary, a former ambassador, is Adjunct Professor at University College Dublin, Ireland.

Lucia Vázquez Mendoza is a postdoctoral researcher in the Department of Sociology, Maynooth University, Ireland.

RELIGION MATTERS: ON THE SIGNIFICANCE OF RELIGION IN GLOBAL ISSUES

Edited by Christine Schliesser, Zurich University, Switzerland, S. Ayse Kadayifci-Orellana, Georgetown University, USA, and Pauline Kollontai, York St. John University, UK.

Policy makers, academics and practitioners worldwide are increasingly paying attention to the role of religion in global issues. This development is clearly noticeable in conflict resolution, development, and climate change, to name just a few pressing issues of global relevance. Up to now, no book series has attempted to analyze the role of religion in current global issues in a coherent and systematic way that pertains to academics, policy makers and practitioners alike. The Sustainable Development Goals (SDGs) serve as a dynamic frame of reference for the series. "Religion Matters" provides cutting edge scholarship in a concise format and accessible language, NB full stop remains at the end of the sentence.

ON THE SIGNIFICANCE OF RELIGION IN CONFLICT AND CONFLICT RESOLUTION
CHRISTINE SCHLIESSER, S. AYSE KADAYIFCI-ORELLANA AND PAULINE KOLLONTAI

ON THE SIGNIFICANCE OF RELIGION FOR GLOBAL DIPLOMACY
PHILIP MCDONAGH, KISHAN MANOCHA, JOHN NEARY AND LUCIA VÁZQUEZ MENDOZA

For more information about this series, please visit:
https://www.routledge.com/religion/series/RELMAT

ON THE SIGNIFICANCE OF RELIGION FOR GLOBAL DIPLOMACY

Philip McDonagh,
Kishan Manocha,
John Neary, and
Lucia Vázquez Mendoza

Routledge
Taylor & Francis Group

LONDON AND NEW YORK

First published 2021
by Routledge
2 Park Square, Milton Park, Abingdon, Oxon OX14 4RN

and by Routledge
52 Vanderbilt Avenue, New York, NY 10017

Routledge is an imprint of the Taylor & Francis Group, an informa business

© 2021 Philip McDonagh, Kishan Manocha, John Neary, and Lucia Vázquez
Mendoza

The right of Philip McDonagh, Kishan Manocha, John Neary, and Lucia Vázquez
Mendoza to be identified as the authors of this work has been asserted by them
in accordance with sections 77 and 78 of the Copyright, Designs and Patents
Act 1988.

The Open Access version of this book, available at www.taylorfrancis.com, has
been made available under a Creative Commons Attribution-Non Commercial-No
Derivatives 4.0 license.

Trademark notice: Product or corporate names may be trademarks or registered
trademarks, and are used only for identification and explanation without intent
to infringe.

British Library Cataloguing-in-Publication Data
A catalogue record for this book is available from the British Library

Library of Congress Cataloging-in-Publication Data
Names: McDonagh, Philip, 1952- author. | Manocha, Kishan, author. | Neary,
John (Foreign Affairs), author. | Vázquez Mendoza, Lucia, author.
Title: On the significance of religion for global diplomacy / Philip
McDonagh, Kishan Manocha, John Neary, Lucia Vázquez Mendoza.
Description: Abingdon, Oxon ; New York, NY : Routledge, 2020. | Series:
Religion matters: on the significance of religion for global issues |
Includes bibliographical references and index.
Identifiers: LCCN 2020029110 | ISBN 9780367514341 (hardback) | ISBN
9780367514358 (paperback) | ISBN 9781003053842 (ebook)
Subjects: LCSH: Religion and politics.
Classification: LCC BL65.P7 M3555 2020 | DDC 201/.727--dc23
LC record available at https://lccn.loc.gov/2020029110

ISBN: 978-0-367-51434-1 (hbk)
ISBN: 978-0-367-51435-8 (pbk)
ISBN: 978-1-003-05384-2 (ebk)

Typeset in Bembo
by SPi Gloal, India

Printed and bound by CPI Group (UK) Ltd, Croydon, CR0 4YY

CONTENTS

NOTES ON THE AUTHORS

Philip McDonagh is Adjunct Professor and Director of the Centre for Religion, Human Values, and International Relations at Dublin City University. In the Department of Foreign Affairs, Philip worked on the Good Friday (Belfast) Agreement and in several multilateral frameworks (EU, UN, OSCE) and developed a strong interest in the intersection of religion and diplomacy as Ambassador in India, Russia, and the Holy See. He has published poetry and plays and written extensively on religion, poetry, and the public sphere. He is Distinguished Global Fellow at the Center of Theological Inquiry (Princeton) and a member of: the Advisory Council of the Institute for Economics and Peace (Sydney); the Steering Committee of the OSCE Academic Network (Hamburg); and the Advisory Council of the Institute for Integrated Transitions (Barcelona).

Kishan Manocha is Head of the Tolerance and Non-Discrimination Department at the OSCE Office for Democratic Institutions and Human Rights in Warsaw. Immediately prior to that he was Senior Adviser on Freedom of Religion or Belief. He has extensive experience in religious freedom and related issues in Europe, the Middle East, North Africa, and Central and South Asia as an advocate, researcher, trainer, and consultant to a number of international and non-governmental organisations. He has been a Visiting Research Fellow at the Carr Centre for Human Rights at Harvard University and a Fellow of the Montreal Institute for Genocide and Human Rights Studies. He is currently Research Fellow at the Religious Freedom and Business Foundation and a Professional Associate at the Centre for Law and Religion at Cardiff University.

John Neary was a diplomat in the Irish Department of Foreign Affairs and Trade from 1974 until his retirement from the Foreign Service in 2016. He served as Ireland's Ambassador to Japan from 2010 to 2014 and as Ambassador to the Netherlands from 2014 until 2016. He is currently a member of the Working Group on the Future of the EU 27 at the Institute of International and European Affairs (IIEA) in Dublin. In 2017, he was appointed Adjunct Professor at University College Dublin where he works to support the University in developing its links with Japan. He is also a member of the Board of Trustees of the Chester Beatty Library in Dublin.

Lucia Vázquez Mendoza received her PhD degree in Sociology from the University of Essex, UK. She is currently a postdoctoral researcher at the Department of Sociology (MUSSI), Maynooth University. Her major research interests are in the field of religious diversity and pluralism in contemporary society. She has conducted ethnographic studies in Pentecostal churches in Mexico and is interested in a broad range of social and anthropological issues. She has participated in multi-disciplinary research projects in Ireland, the United Kingdom, France, and Mexico.

ACKNOWLEDGEMENTS

This book has its origins in a number of particular circumstances.

On my retirement from the Department of Foreign Affairs in 2017, Peter Cassells, then Director of the Kennedy Institute at the National University of Ireland Maynooth, Peter's Assistant Director, Kieran Doyle, and Fr. Michael Shortall, Registrar of St. Patrick's College Maynooth, invited me to develop a module for graduate students on religion, peace, and diplomacy. John Neary, Kishan Manocha, and Lucia Vázquez Mendoza were colleagues in delivering this module.

In 2018, Kishan played a key role in a research project that I convened within the OSCE academic network with the participation of several distinguished academics and 'practitioners'. This project was supported by the Kennedy Institute, St. Patrick's College, and the Irish, Swiss, and Austrian Departments of Foreign Affairs. A report was presented to the OSCE participating states in January 2019, under the title 'Religion and Security-Building in the OSCE Context: Involving Religious Leaders and Congregations in Joint Efforts' (this report can be accessed on the website of the OSCE Network of Think Tanks and Academic Institutions).

Christine Schliesser and Pauline Kollontai, two of the three editors of the series 'Religion Matters', were my colleagues at the Center of Theological Inquiry at Princeton in the spring semester of 2019. Christine, Pauline, and their fellow series editor, S. Ayse Kadayifci-Orellana, invited me to join their advisory board and to work on the present collaborative volume, taking the OSCE report and the module on religion, peace, and diplomacy as points of departure. Without this imaginative outreach on their part to someone who, up to now, has been primarily a 'practitioner', this work would not have been undertaken. John, Kishan, Lucia, and I have once again worked closely together. Mutual moral support has been as important a factor as varied expertise.

In 2020, at the invitation of the incoming President of Dublin City University (DCU), Professor Daire Keogh, I have started developing a Centre for Religion, Human Values, and International Relations at DCU, working closely with Professor John Doyle, Dean of the Faculty of Humanities, and Professor Brad Anderson, Head of the Faculty of Theology, Philosophy, and Music. This book has taken shape alongside the development of the DCU Centre.

The ideas in the book depend on many conversations, including, of course, among the co-authors. I would like to acknowledge a number of specific debts to those who helped in some way or another to bring this book project to fruition.

Fionnuala Croke, Director of that wonderful Dublin institution, the Chester Beatty, and her whole team, including Dr. Moya Carey, the Curator for Islamic Manuscripts, have been of great assistance to us in delivering the module on religion, peace, and diplomacy. The Chester Beatty embodies the values that inspired this book. Maynooth's University Library, the John Paul II Library, has also very kindly hosted some of our classes. Ciara Joyce of the Library staff is a guest contributor to this volume with a short essay based on the Ken Saro-Wiwa papers which are housed in the Library.

My late uncle, Rev. Professor Feichín O'Doherty, was a brilliant and adventurous theologian, a pioneering professor of psychology, and a quietly passionate advocate of reform in several spheres. Some of his thinking has found its way into this volume. In particular, our first axiom, that *we should examine the patterns of our behaviour in the light of all that we ought to know and can know*, is based on so-far unpublished notes of Feichín of which I am the custodian.

Another 'oral tradition' that finds its way into this book is that of the Church of Scotland. In the course of several conversations,

Dr. William Storrar, Director of the Center of Theological Inquiry, has enabled me to grasp something of the thought of J. H. Oldham. Before and during World War II, Oldham began exploring the concept of 'middle axioms' as a possible bridge between theology and politics. This is the initial spark that led to our 'axioms of the historical imagination' espoused in this book. In preparing this book, we found our way by a separate route to the thinking of Helmuth von Moltke's Kreisau Circle, briefly referred to in Chapter 5. It seems appropriate to remember here the wartime contacts in Switzerland between the friends of Oldham and the friends of von Moltke.

As the guest of Princeton's University Center for Human Values (UCHV), I had the privilege of many illuminating conversations with Joseph Chan. Joseph enabled me to see that the 'structural questions' facing political philosophy in China and Europe are analogous; from this, a cross-cultural dialogue follows easily. To an old family friend, the great historian Romila Thapar, I owe the insight that the Shramana dharma in India is, among other things, a tradition of dissent. This helps explain the thinking of several of India's prophetic figures, as well as the often generous response within Indian society to pathfinding political ideas.

I owe to Joel Rosenthal, Director of the Carnegie Council for Ethics in International Affairs, the insight that the multifarious phenomena of globalisation can be organised under the three main headings of nature, the virtual world, and politics.

Virgil's Aeneas seems often to be in need of external affirmation as he journeys towards the Ausonian fields that ever recede before him (see Chapter 4 of this book). In late 2019, I benefited greatly from an invitation from Professor Peter Ochs to teach at the University of Virginia (UVA). The goals we pursue in this book are in harmony, or so I hope, with Peter's work over many decades in developing 'scriptural reasoning'. Peter's colleague at UVA, the American diplomat Jerry White, has done work of worldwide significance in the campaign to ban landmines and on behalf of persons with disabilities – outstanding case studies in how the leaven of human values can transform multilateral diplomacy.

John, Kishan, Lucia, and I have been fortunate in our reader and adviser in South Africa, Lee-Anne Roux, and in the warm, friendly, and patient encouragement of the team at Routledge led by Rebecca Shillabeer and Amy Doffegnies. We are grateful to artist Regina Baumhauer for another exquisite cover image for this series.

When we propose that international organisations should use their convening power to bring about new, multilayered, consultative processes, inclusive of the representatives of religion, our premise is that religion and human values are at one. On the cold morning of 30 May 1955, 65 years ago today, Vasily Grossman climbed the stairs to the first floor of the Pushkin Museum to view Raphael's painting *The Sistine Madonna*. Grossman's response to the painting, written in 1955, was published only in 1989:

> Every epoch contemplates this woman with a child in her arms, and a tender, moving, and sorrowful sense of brotherhood comes into being between people of different generations, nations, races, and eras. Conscious now of themselves and the cross they must bear, people suddenly understand the miraculous links between different ages, the way everything that has ever lived and will live is linked to what is living now ... And the painting also tells us how precious, how splendid life has to be and that no force in the world can compel life to change into some other thing that, however it may resemble life, is no longer life. (Vasily Grossman. (2010). 'The Sistine Madonna,' in *The Road: Short Fiction and Essays* (translated by Robert and Elizabeth Chandler with Olga Mukovnika), pp. 185–186, 191. London: Maclehose Press)

Philip McDonagh
Dublin
30 May 2020

ACKNOWLEDGEMENT
OF COVER ARTIST

Cover photo: Regina Baumhauer,
Open Letter, Dr. Zhivago, 2012; oil, graphite, and
acrylics on canvas;
120 cm × 120 cm/48″ × 48″;
New York, June, 2020;
https://rbaumhauer.wixsite.com/reginabaumhauer

ABBREVIATIONS

AI	Artificial intelligence
ASEAN	Association of Southeast Asian Nations
AU	African Union
AU-IFDF	African Union Interfaith Dialogue Forum
CBM	Confidence-building measure
CFR	Council on Foreign Relations
CITES	Convention on the International Trade in Endangered Species of Wild Flora and Fauna
CoE	Council of Europe
CPP	Collective Psychology Project
CSCE	Conference on Security and Cooperation in Europe
DCU	Dublin City University
EC	European Commission
EP	European Parliament
EU	European Union
FBO	Faith-based organisation
FRA	Fundamental Rights Agency
GATT	General Agreement on Trade and Tariffs
GDP	Gross domestic product
GDPR	General Data Protection Regulation

HCHF	Higher Committee of Human Fraternity
ICCPR	International Covenant on Civil and Political Rights
ICJ	International Court of Justice
IEP	Institute for Economics and Peace
IIEA	Institute of International and European Affairs
IPSP	International Panel on Social Progress
LoN	League of Nations
MDGs	Millennium Development Goals
MOSOP	Movement for the Survival of the Ogoni People
MUSSI	Maynooth University Social Sciences Institute
NGO	Non-governmental organisation
NPT	Nuclear Non-Proliferation Treaty
OAS	Organization of American States
ODA	Overseas development assistance
ODIHR	Office for Democratic Institutions and Human Rights
OECD	Organisation for Economic Cooperation and Development
OHCHR	Office of the United Nations High Commissioner for Human Rights
OLA	Missionary Sisters of Our Lady of the Apostles
OPCW	Organisation for the Prohibition of Chemical Weapons
OSCE	Organisation for Security and Cooperation in Europe
PaRD	International Partnership on Religion and Sustainable Development
PRC	Pew Research Center
RfP	Religions for Peace
SAARC	South Asian Association for Regional Cooperation
SDG	Sustainable development goal
TFEU	Treaty on the Functioning of the European Union
UCHV	University Center for Human Values
UDHR	Universal Declaration of Human Rights
UK	United Kingdom
UN	United Nations
UNCTAD	United Nations Conference on Trade and Development

UNDP	United Nations Development Program
UNEP	United Nations Environment Programme
UNESCO	United Nations Educational, Scientific and Cultural Organization
UNFCCC	United Nations Framework Convention on Climate Change
UNHCR	UN High Commissioner for Refugees
UN-IATF	United Nations Inter-Agency Task Force
UNICEF	United Nations Children's Fund
US	United States
UVA	University of Virginia
WHO	World Health Organization
WTO	World Trade Organization

SUMMARY AND RECOMMENDATIONS TO GOVERNMENTS, INTERNATIONAL ORGANISATIONS, AND CIVIL SOCIETY

On the Significance of Religion for Global Diplomacy is an exercise of the historical imagination. We start from current realities: pandemic, climate change and environmental degradation, the impact of digital technologies, and widening social disparities. The future is invisible, indeterminate, and full of risk. It often seems that history is accelerating. What is to be done? Is there a guiding principle? Is there a next step?

In 2020, public authorities are making significant value judgements as they respond to the novel coronavirus (COVID-19). Well-being means more than economic growth. State intervention is part of the solution. For their part, citizens are making sacrifices for the community; the term 'front line' is acquiring a new meaning. All over the world, we glimpse new horizons, even in the literal sense, as pollution lifts. A dialogue is developing on the extent of our interdependence and how it is best managed.

In late March 2020, the UN Secretary General called for a 'global ceasefire'. A ceasefire is usually the prelude to talks, negotiations, and a peace treaty. If state and non-state actors were to suspend, or seriously qualify, the immediate struggle for advantage in order to capture the lessons learned in the pandemic, what could or should happen next? The state of global politics invites us to rethink the economy and the nature of international security – an epochal challenge. This book argues for a specific intermediate step in the realm of methodology and orientation.

Freedom of religion or belief is a core value in our societies. 'Religious literacy' is already acknowledged as a necessary diplomatic skill. It is time to enable a deeper engagement by public authorities with religious perspectives as a resource in global peacebuilding and diplomacy. 'Social capital' and other features of a strong political culture are also a primary focus of the world's religions.

Our recommendations can be summarised as follows:

1. We can develop 'axioms of the historical imagination' to provide a common criterion of evaluation across cultures and from one situation to another. Acting in the light of common axioms creates community, even among people and groups who never interact directly.
2. We propose the following axioms:
   * we should examine the patterns of our behaviour in the light of all that we ought to know and can know
   * we should 'image' or visualise peace as the rightful possession of the human community as a whole
   * we should identify and explore the factors that accompany healing in a wounded social structure
   * we should recognise that the starting position for political deliberation is inevitably non-ideal
   * discernment in the midst of opacity in accordance with a common standard should become a core value in the conduct of international relations
   * we should give expression to a changing diplomatic culture through new frameworks of engagement
3. In particular, international organisations should use their convening power to bring about new, multilayered, consultative processes, inclusive of the representatives of religion, as an extra dimension within the wider project of making multilateral

diplomacy fit-for-purpose. These new processes will under-pin the implementation of the United Nations Sustainable Development Goals (SDGs) and complement the day-to-day negotiations that currently take place in a range of diplomatic settings. New consultative processes will require a new style of negotiating mandate aimed at a distinctive diplomatic 'product'.

4. This 'product' will be a combination of (i) the gradual definition of new criteria or points of agreement to govern the conduct of international relations and (ii) confidence-building measures (CBMs) with *demonstration value* in the perspective of a future 'age of sharing' at the global level.

5. We examine criteria for the effective interaction of policymakers with religious actors. The religions can use the dialogue with public authorities to their own advantage to start new discussions or initiatives on issues of social justice.

6. Our axioms point towards an 'anthropological' development over the coming decades – a global humanism founded on a broad understanding of the scope of reason. A richer understanding of the meaning of freedom is central to this new humanism.

In our Introduction, we discuss the present point of inflection in world history. In Chapter 1, we propose that the conversation about the future should begin with a series of structural questions that arise independently of any one religious or philosophical tradition. Chapters 2–6 develop the axioms that in our view can interact with specialised competencies across all the relevant subject areas of mul-tilateral diplomacy. In an inherently pluralist global society, we can mark off the essential common ground.

Our central thesis is that new forms of historical and religious literacy, allied to new frameworks of engagement, can enable a more creative global diplomacy. The Epilogue illustrates our recommen-dations in a practical way, by presenting a brief outline of what an all-European initiative might look like if, in the early 2020s, there were the political will to inaugurate a long-term, multilayered, value-oriented, regional, diplomatic process accessible to citizens.

Engaging the religions within a culture of dialogue or encoun-ter can transform our understanding of effective action and give us the courage to undertake the difficult journey into the future in shared hope, *as if a merciful God exists*. This decision, or disposition, can become, in the French phrase, *le provisoire qui dure* ('the provisional that lasts'); a hypothesis can become a habit. Here lies a viable 21st-century alternative to the 'law of the strongest' in international relations.

INTRODUCTION

TOWARDS A CULTURE OF ENCOUNTER INCLUSIVE OF THE WORLD'S RELIGIOUS TRADITIONS

A POINT OF INFLECTION

On many issues, the global consensus is broken. Severe new challenges are emerging. Power relations are shifting. The economic productivity associated with globalisation has not translated into a shared confidence in the future.

The President of the US Council on Foreign Relations (CFR) speaks guardedly: 'The gap between the challenges generated by globalisation and the ability of a world to cope with them appears to be widening in a number of critical domains … centrifugal forces are gaining the upper hand' (Haass, 2017, pp. 11–12). Pope Francis is blunt: 'We can see signs that things are now reaching a breaking point … the present world system is certainly unsustainable from a number of points of view … Doomsday predictions can no longer be met with irony or disdain' (*Laudato Si'*, 2015).

As we write this Introduction in spring 2020, the following is a random selection of recent, mainstream book titles alerting us to the dangers we face: *How Democracies Die* (Levitsky and Ziblatt, 2018), *Living Well at Others' Expense: The Hidden Costs of Western Prosperity* (Lessenich, 2019), *Licence to Be Bad: How Economics Corrupted Us* (Aldred, 2019), and *Don't Be Evil: The Case against Big Tech* (Foroohar, 2019). Common to these and many other similar studies is a sense that the cohesion of our societies is threatened by a deficit in the realm of values. Under 21st-century conditions, any deficit in this realm is, in large part, an international question. Whether a sense of community continues to attract and animate a multiplicity of actors, at home and abroad, opening the door to common action is ultimately a 'civilisational' or 'anthropological' question.

In our globalised 21st century, we have reached a point of inflection in the human story. One way or another, our policy responses will depend on the lens through which we see reality. How do we see the relationship between the citizen and the state? How do we measure the economy? Is building community compatible with individuals advancing their own self-interests? Should we protect the vulnerable? Are we global citizens? What position do we take on questions concerning human origins, human destiny, and our place within nature? In thinking about politics, how do we answer the basic questions: who, where, how, why, and when (Lane, 2014, pp. 11–17)?

LEARNING FROM 19TH-CENTURY EUROPE

As we enter the unscripted future, the world community of the 21st century can learn from the study of 19th-century Europe. In the 19th century, long-term contradictions in political thinking created vulnerabilities – an ethical and cultural deficit in European society – that in conjunction with other, more immediate, factors, led to World War I. The contradictions to which we refer have their roots in a vision of progress in which interpersonal relationships and a sense of shared well-being are thought to be less important than innovation, competition, the mobilisation of power, and conceptions of national destiny (Arendt, 1951). For European elites, it was easier to mobilise populations for war than to withdraw from empire or to address the 'social question' that was presenting itself with such urgency in each European jurisdiction.

Today, once again, though in a different way than in the 19th century, the pursuit of advantage (technological, financial, military) by rival governments and corporations weakens our shared sense of the common good; our way of life as countries and as individuals is often highly competitive and is marked by huge disparities; and our sense of 'belonging' has not kept pace with higher living standards for many and a dramatic overall increase in population, resources, and capabilities.

Other changes magnify the danger. We continue to destroy the natural environment. We have experienced a financial crisis. We are exposed to epidemics such as SARS and pandemics such as COVID-19; more new diseases are inevitable, given mutations in the microbial world and the way we inhabit the planet. Our highly organised societies are vulnerable to cyberattack. Technological advances, such as interventions in the human genome and the uses of artificial intelligence (if 'intelligence' is the right word for the mathematical analysis of accumulated data), are changing how we think about human freedom and dignity. Our weapons of mass destruction are at best 'stranded assets'. In many larger countries, the arms industry and the arms trade are taken as much for granted as in the days when the mass production and aggressive marketing of the Maxim gun was supposedly making war less likely.

In the present century, though the stakes are even higher than in 1914, the techniques of marketing, applied to politics, undermine debate and engagement. Access to information and to the means of communication is accompanied in many cases by an absence of perspective. We often turn to national narratives that offer an easy escape from complexity. Arguably, there is no space at the global level within which to listen to others and to develop, without pre-conceptions, a 'shared vocabulary of justice' (Hurrell, 2007, p. 303).

TOWARDS AN ENABLING ENVIRONMENT FOR LONG-TERM EVOLUTIONARY CHANGE

In the crisis of 2020, public authorities have made significant moral judgements. Saving lives is more important than economic growth. Higher levels of public spending and state intervention can serve the common good. A coherent public health strategy requires international cooperation. We, the public, have made sacrifices for the sake of the community. Many ordinary citizens, including, of course, healthcare professionals, have displayed the courage of soldiers in wartime. The volunteers coming forward in huge numbers are not 'incentivised' by money. In many parts of the world, we have glimpsed new horizons, even in the literal sense, as pollution has lifted, and blue skies and distant mountain tops have become visible for the first time in many years.

The UN Sustainable Development Goals, adopted by consensus by more than 190 states in 2015, represent, in embryo, a vision of the global citizenship of nation states and a medium-term common plan for humanity that takes into account the 'density' of interactions across borders and the interconnectedness of issues. The Global Compact for Migration, adopted in 2018, rests in part on the 2030 Agenda for Sustainable Development framed by the sustainable development goals (SDGs). Similar values underpin the United Nations Framework Convention on Climate Change (UNFCCC) and the work of the World Health Organization (WHO) in bringing COVID-19 under control.

Our actions during the pandemic, added to the thinking that has gone into multilateral diplomacy over the past decade, signify that many people are ready to convert the present point of inflection, or crisis, into an opportunity – a springboard to a global project that can empower the 'better angels of our nature' in the perspective of 2030 or 2050. As an Indian writer and activist puts it: 'The world is literally gasping for breath. We all need a new kind of oxygen – a new design for living' (Thapar, 2020, n.p.).

In this book we propose introducing or reintroducing to the world of multilateral diplomacy the explicit questions: What do we believe in? What is our 'design for living'? To answer these questions means drawing on dimensions of our lives that do not originate in the public sphere: 'The formal political structures of our time are incapable of confronting this crisis on their own' (Ghosh, 2016, p. 214).

As the catalyst for a civilisational transformation, we propose a *culture of encounter inclusive of the world's religious traditions*, to be enabled by international organisations. We see this as a long-term cross-cultural enterprise with roots in civil society. It is an enterprise fully congruent with the UN's new emphasis on mobilising civil society to sustain peace.

Good conceptual work in an 'agora', or several agoras, of the kind described in this book can help create an enabling environment for long-term evolutionary change without calling into question governments' ability to defend immediate interests in day-to-day negotiations elsewhere. That is to say, our proposal aims to complement, not replace, the specialised negotiations that go forward in a range of diplomatic settings – for example, budgetary negotiations within the European Union (EU), arms control negotiations between the US and Russia (or in future, between the US, Russia, and China?), dispute settlement within the World Trade Organization (WTO), and follow up to the SDGs, the Global Compact for Migration, and the Convention on Climate Change. New consultative processes will require a new style of mandate: long-term, inclusive, regional, multilayered, accessible to citizens, and aimed at a distinctive diplomatic 'product'. We develop these criteria in detail in Chapter 6.

WHY PUBLIC AUTHORITIES SHOULD ENGAGE WITH A RELIGIOUS PERSPECTIVE

Why is it potentially so fruitful for public authorities to engage with a religious perspective? Our answer relates to the role of *knowledge* in the policy-making process – which we will now examine briefly from four angles: religious literacy, collective psychology, moral discernment, and personal communication. These themes will be developed further throughout the book.

RELIGIOUS LITERACY

The first point on our list is religious literacy. Religion is a dimension of experience and practice that matters greatly to many people and cannot be entirely reduced to other factors. In the 21st century, worldwide, the importance of religion in society is not diminishing. The Pew Research Center (PRC) in Washington, DC is a key source of information. According to a 2015 PRC report, Christians were the largest religious group in the world in that same year, making up nearly a third (31%) of the earth's 7.3 billion people. Muslims were second, with 1.8 billion people, or 24% of the global population, followed by Hindus (15%) and Buddhists (7%). Jews and members of other religions make up smaller shares of the world's people. Those professing no religion were a minority (16%). Between 2015 and 2060, the world's population is expected to increase by 32% to 9.6 billion. The religious landscape may change; it may include, for example, a greater proportion of Muslims. The point to register, for present purposes, is that in the year 2050, to which this book looks forward, 80% or more of the world's population are likely to profess a religious faith.

These broad-brush figures fail to reveal many important distinctions. We acknowledge that over three centuries there has been a draining of cultural energy from the great religions of the West.

This has impacted in turn on religious education in that great part of the globe that was colonised. Arguably, therefore, religion remains a strong source of personal motivation in the 21st century under conditions in which religious learning, interreligious dialogue, and the dialogue of public authorities with religion have been undervalued over a long period (Ochs, 2019).

In recent years, in a partial change of direction, 'religious literacy' and 'faith-based diplomacy' have been increasingly recognised as essential areas of expertise. With a view to conflict prevention and conflict resolution, diplomats aim to understand the significance of religion within the political economy of a country or a region (Johnston, 2003). In many situations, 'religious literacy' is absolutely essential for policy-making, even if religion, as such, is not necessarily a root cause – take, for example, Northern Ireland, Israel and the Palestinians, the politics of the Indian subcontinent, the rivalry between Iran and Saudi Arabia, the case of the Uighurs in China, the rise of movements such as al-Qaeda (initially with the involvement of Western intelligence agencies), Russian–Ukrainian relations, the role of Pentecostalism in Latin America, and the electoral politics of the US.

Many important political concepts can only be understood fully by a 'religiously literate' observer; for example, the sacredness of the earth in the eyes of indigenous peoples, ahimsa or non-violence in the Indian tradition, the caliphate in Islam, and in every tradition, the nuances of mercy, reconciliation, and forgiveness.

Up to a generation ago, social thinkers often assumed that 'modernisation' implied the 'disenchantment of the world' and the decline of religion. Today, we see clearly that the 21st-century landscape is defined, not by *secularisation*, but by *pluralism*. We agree with the 2018 report of the International Panel on Social Progress (IPSP):

> Social progress depends on establishing civil societies where people of diverse heritage can not only work and live together, but also flourish in each other's company. Each society, moreover, must find a way forward within the parameters set by its past. For this reason, progress will look different in different places.
>
> (Davie et al., 2018, pp. 641–676)

COLLECTIVE PSYCHOLOGY

The salience of religion in the political economy of many parts of the world leads us to our second point. The major features of a strong political culture are also a primary focus of the world's religions.

The Collective Psychology Project (CPP) was started at New York University in 2018. It relies, in part, on the following empirical observations:

> First, religion has over recent centuries retreated steadily from the public sphere in the west and become seen as a purely private concern ... Second, more recently, religiosity itself has been in steep decline in most developed countries, especially among the young. The result of these two epochal shifts is that, almost unnoticed, one of our most important spaces for the practice of collective psychology, over thousands of years, has been eroding steadily, leaving a vacuum in its wake.
>
> (CPP, 2018, p. 14)

Because there is no clear frontier separating our inner, psychological lives, on the one hand, and our outer, real world lives, on the other, the trend identified by the CPP poses a risk to society:

> We used to think depression and anxiety were just about brain chemistry, for example. Now, though, we're realizing that they have deep roots in the ways our culture fails to meet psychological needs for many – and perhaps most – of us.
>
> (CPP, 2018, p. 8)

But is the CPP on completely solid ground? Are the two 'epochal shifts' in 'most developed countries' decisive for humanity as a whole, or even for Europe and America? Instead of relying only on psychology to fill the void left by the decline of religion, what if public authorities began to engage creatively with the world's religious traditions in order to draw out their acknowledged capacity to foster collective self-awareness, a collective sense of agency, and a collective sense of belonging?

To accept limits for the sake of the common interest; to act separately yet pull together in complex environments; to trust others; to have the energy and hope to face the future – these features of the global response to the COVID-19 pandemic are close to being an exact description of a living religious faith.

MORAL DISCERNMENT

The third point on our list is that religious communities can make a further vital contribution to global diplomacy by insisting that within the opacity of political situations there is always a better path, however imperfect or 'provisional' that better option may be. Specifically, a cross-disciplinary engagement with *religion and human values* can shed light on structural factors – political and economic – that amount to an abdication of responsibility towards future generations or to the 'domination' (Pettit, 2014, p. 207) of some groups by others.

For the prophets of the Bible, the failure of government is a form of untruth which weighs on the poor, the oppressed, the humble of the earth, and those in need. 'Trouble is coming to the man who builds a city in bloodshed and makes it great in the midst of injustices' (Habakkuk 2:12).[1] Not might, nor power, but the 'Spirit of God' sustains a peaceful society (Zechariah 4:6b; cf. 12:10). The biblical question concerning the need for a change of *heart* that changes *society* (Jonah in Nineveh, John the Baptist in Roman Palestine) is posed in a comparable way in other world civilisations. According to the Way (*Dao*) of Confucius, leaders are at the service of the people in seeking to align current conditions with an ethical, social, and political ideal. In ancient India, Ashoka's vision is of a world founded on dharma, a way of life in conformity with truth. The close link between our personal lives and the character of the age is brought out by Jesus: 'with the burgeoning of false law (*anomia*), love will grow cold in most people' (Matthew 24:12).

The interplay between the material and spiritual dimensions of life as the basis for human flourishing and discernment is repeatedly emphasised in the Baha'i Writings, for example, in the following passage from 'Abdu'l-Bahá (1982, p. 16):

> No matter how far the material world advances, it cannot establish the happiness of mankind. Only when material and spiritual civilization are linked and coordinated will happiness be assured.

In the European classical world, an education in *humanitas* was considered the best preparation for public life (Marrou, 1958).

Humanitas, a term coined by Cicero, suggests both sympathy for all fellow human beings and openness towards every department of knowledge. The Italian Renaissance begins with Petrarch's discovery of Cicero. For the 'humanists', there is no dichotomy between 'the material' and 'the spiritual'; and there is no inherent conflict between the products of culture and the insights of religion. The educational ideals of Erasmus, who, like Petrarch, was a religious believer, are centred on *humanitas* and *pietas* – *pietas* here signifying a religious upbringing.

We need to picture more clearly the *educational formation* that will give men and women the capability to understand 'the interplay between the material and spiritual dimensions of life', matching vision with concrete responsibilities, and connecting one issue to another across cultures and thematic areas. Our 'axioms of the historical imagination' are intended as a contribution to this new humanism. The danger to be avoided is a disconnect between the public sphere and particular domains of knowledge and activity.

PERSONAL COMMUNICATION

Our fourth angle on a 'post-secular sensitivity' in global diplomacy is that it will have implications for the personal interactions of diplomats and for the informal consultations and academic contributions that underpin 'track one' diplomacy.

During the Cold War, the Jewish philosopher Martin Buber[2] identified the prevalence of 'existential mistrust' among diplomats. At that time, American diplomats could not imagine that their understanding of the world would be altered in any way by an encounter with a Soviet counterpart. As we look back at the circumstances of the early 1950s, we find this understandable; a situation in which diplomats live constantly on the 'official' level, acting out a part, may sometimes be unavoidable. In the long run, however, 'existential mistrust' of adversaries and their supposedly monolithic bureaucracies cannot offer a pathway to collective agency at the global level. Diplomacy becomes a game of power, resembling the interaction of physical systems.

For many-sided negotiations to bear fruit, personal interactions are a prerequisite. Diplomats must have the freedom to undertake exploratory discussions with counterparts with a view to understanding their points of view, the dangers they fear, whether they consider that changes of position can occur, and where they see the possibility of new beginnings. In other words, we expect diplomatic contacts to enable the interaction, not of physical, but of moral, systems. This requires us to bring words and their real meanings into play. The 'personal, human level', including especially trust, becomes all-important.

In *Laudato Si'*, Pope Francis sees the current state of the world through the lens of climate change. Having presented the evidence, Pope Francis wants us to make the transition from seeing to suffering:

> Our goal is not to amass information or satisfy curiosity but rather to become painfully aware, to dare to turn what is happening in our world into our own personal suffering and thus to discover what each of us can do about it.
>
> (*Laudato Si'*, 2015, 19)

This vital aspect of the personal in diplomacy – the painful awareness that we are not in a 'good place' and that we are not in control of the future – naturally reinforces dialogue as a political value. Our need draws us closer together.

Martin Buber makes a concrete proposal to address 'existential mistrust' among diplomats. Representatives having the confidence of their respective groups, but capable at the same time of independent thought, should somehow be brought together to try to find common ground (in Mittleman, 2009, p. 228). This book takes up Buber's vision. A future values-led dialogue at the international level should be conducted by men and women who bring something of themselves to the conference room, and who learn to trust one another – whether they be responsible officials, trusted representatives of religious communities, business leaders, or other actors in civil society. Spokespersons of all kinds will need both specialised knowledge and 'historical and religious literacy' – they will need *humanitas*.

Interreligious dialogue can help prepare the way for a better style of global diplomacy. The form of interreligious dialogue most suited to our diplomatic project is 'scriptural reasoning' (Ochs, 2019). Scriptural reasoning encourages each tradition to look more deeply into its own deepest sources. Without denying religious pluralism, this form of reasoning aims to build relationships and improve the quality of dialogue ('the quality of our disagreements').

Even more saliently, scriptural reasoning enables its practitioners to look at contemporary challenges, including diplomatic and political challenges, with a view to new commitments and new forms of collaboration.

BUILDING ON EXISTING FOUNDATIONS

Our proposal for public authorities to engage with a religious perspective through new frameworks of engagement builds on existing foundations. Freedom of religion or belief, a core human rights principle, is not compatible with the relegation of religion to what happens in private. Under the International Covenant on Civil and Political Rights (ICCPR, 1976, Article 18):

> Everyone shall have the right to freedom of thought, conscience, and religion. This right shall include freedom to have or to adopt a religion or belief of his choice, and freedom, either individually or in community with others and *in public or private*, to manifest his religion or belief *in worship, observance, practice and teaching*. (Emphasis added)

In the UN, the Organisation for Security and Cooperation in Europe (OSCE), the EU, and other regional frameworks, mandates allowing for a dialogue between public authorities and the religious confessions are already to a large extent in place. The Treaty on the Functioning of the European Union (TFEU) Article 17(1) provides:

1. The Union respects and does not prejudice the status under national law of churches and religious associations or communities in the Member States.
2. The Union equally respects the status under national law of philosophical and non-confessional organisations.
3. Recognising their identity and their specific contribution, the Union shall maintain an open, transparent and regular dialogue with these churches and organisations.

The Council of Europe (CoE), in the context of a programme of work on 'building inclusive societies together', has promoted a series of 'exchanges' on the religious dimension of intercultural dialogue. The background documentation recognises that a 'pan-European approach to the issue of building inclusive societies' can be supported by 'different approaches' to the role and place of religion in the public space, because of differences in historical, cultural, social, and political circumstances (document RENC (2015)3/28 October 2015).

Meeting in Kiev in 2013, the Ministerial Council of the OSCE (OSCE, 2013) called on participating states to 'encourage the inclusion of religious and belief communities, in a timely fashion, in public discussions of pertinent legislative initiatives'.

In 2019, the Office for Democratic Institutions and Human Rights (ODIHR), an institution of the OSCE, published policy guidance for the states of the OSCE region. Included in their guidelines are a wide range of recommendations; of particular interest here are the following:

> Participating States are encouraged to promote and facilitate initiatives of interfaith and inter-religious dialogue and partnership at all levels of society …
>
> Participating States should establish permanent channels of communication and/or focal points at national, regional and local levels to build trust with representatives of different religious or belief communities.
>
> (OSCE/ODIHR, 2019, pp. 48–49)

Previously, ODIHR had published (with the Venice Commission) Guidelines on the Legal Personality of Religious or Belief Communities (OSCE/ODIHR, 2014).

Another indication of changing perspectives is that the EUs Fundamental Rights Agency (FRA) is beginning to explore how people motivated by religion and people motivated by human rights can become better partners in shaping fair and just societies.

In the last few years, to cite three key examples, the UN, the African Union (AU), and the G20 have established mechanisms to encourage interfaith dialogue and have the benefit of advice and support from religious leaders and actors (the United Nations Inter-Agency Task Force (UN-IATF) on Religion and Development, the African Union Interfaith Dialogue Forum (AU-IFDF), and the G20 Interfaith Forum).

There is a growing appreciation that mobilising communities in support of social objectives is often much easier when public authorities and religious communities work together. The United Nations Environment Programme (UNEP) promotes the Faith for Earth Initiative (UNEP, 2020), with a mission to engage with faith-based organisations (FBOs) as partners in fulfilling the 2030 Agenda (SDGs). An International Partnership on Religion and Sustainable

Development (PaRD) was established in 2016; PaRD has an impressive reach within civil society. In April 2020, Religions for Peace (RfP) and the United Nations Children's Fund (UNICEF) launched a global Multi-Religious Faith-in-Action COVID-19 Initiative (Joint Learning Initiative on Faith & Local Communities, 2020). These developments at the international level have their counterpart in many individual countries. France, a pioneer of the 'separation of church and state', is also a pioneer of new forms of dialogue between the state and religious communities. In a speech at the Collège des Bernardins in 2018, French President Emmanuel Macron asked the religious confessions to bring 'to the service of the republic' their wisdom, their commitment, and their freedom to speak out (Macron, 2018).

AGENDAS FOR DIALOGUE

An 'open, transparent and regular dialogue' with religious communities can help each society to resolve questions at the intersection of freedom of religion or belief and public policy. ODIHR's policy guidance focuses on issues of relevance in the sphere of security policy, such as the registration of religious communities and the definition of 'extremist' speech and literature. Other delicate issues at the intersection of religious freedom and public policy include education (Article 18, paragraph 4, of the Covenant), the display of symbols, the observance of holidays, and the recognition of religious marriages.

Religious communities in all parts of the world have 'social capital'. They are motivated by their faith to: run schools, hospitals, and charities; engage in development projects; champion human rights; establish community-based media; build bridges across social divisions; and, in general, come to the assistance of the vulnerable. Public authorities have every reason to bring religious communities into practical partnerships, as we have discussed above – a further and very fruitful area for dialogue.

'Faith-based diplomacy' in situations of conflict is already developing strongly. There is a natural complementarity between preventing conflict, educating for peace, and illuminating and motivating the broader politics of global peaceful transformation (Bettiza, 2019, pp. 174–206). However, the existing channels for dialogue between government representatives and the religious communities, though welcome and worthwhile, are not, in them-selves, a broad pathway to a 'civilisational' or 'anthropological' trans-formation in which the secular and the religious interact creatively in the public sphere. That is why we explore a possible step-change in global diplomacy.

DRAWING ON THE BEST OF DIPLOMACY POST-WORLD WAR II

The recommendations that we put forward in this book are aimed partly at recovering a way of seeing the world that was common in the mid-20th century. During and after World War II, resistance to National Socialism in Germany, plans for the welfare state in Britain, and forward thinking in several countries about the post-war world were inspired to a large extent by leaders who were religious believ-ers or whose pursuit of justice was based on a life stance, such as a commitment to socialism. The challenge was to find a commonly accepted language for higher values deeply held.

Though we should not romanticise the motives of the great powers, the international institutions developed in the aftermath of World War II contain 'in their DNA' a place for values, morality, ethics, and justice. They take for granted that governments should address the problems that face humankind as a whole.

In peacebuilding projects, such as the Northern Ireland peace process, and on a grander scale, the reconciliation of France and Germany in the interests of peace in Europe, the discernment of a new political path has always been much more than a matter of technical proficiency.

In the second half of the 20th century, wealthier countries began to provide overseas development assistance (ODA) and to submit their aid performance to peer review. It was widely accepted that good governance implies 'policies and systems that promote social partnership and cohesion' (OSCE, 2003).

In the 21st century, a well-constructed dialogue engaging, in the right way, with religious and philosophical thought, can enable us to bring into play the same traditions of thought and the same *depth* of cultural sources on which we were able to draw in the mid-20th century.

To engender a civilisation of hope, we need to do even more than was done then. We need to engage with qualitatively new challenges and a broader range of dialogue partners and cultural sources – China, for example, is an increasingly important partner. We need to use new forms of knowledge. We need a richer understanding of the terms 'religion', 'secular', and the 'public sphere'. Religious communities should act responsibly, acknowledging that political, social, and juridical arrangements are amenable to reason and debate. Public authorities should understand and recognise the different standpoints and responsibilities of religious communities.

MISUSES OF RELIGION

In many situations, the dislocations caused by globalisation are cementing the significance of religion in a problematic manner. This is especially the case in situations of political polarisation (or 'radicalisation'). Religion, or a worldview with 'religious' characteristics, can serve as a marker of group identity; as a means of removing a political issue from the realm of critical scrutiny; or as an obstacle to integration, whether of people or of ideas.

In February 2019, Pope Francis and the Grand Imam of Al-Azhar, Sheikh Ahmed el-Tayeb, issued a joint 'Document on Human Fraternity for World Peace and Living Together' (Higher Committee of Human Fraternity (HCHF), 2019). This document addresses the misuses of religion:

> We resolutely declare that religions must never incite war, hateful attitudes, hostility and extremism, nor must they incite violence or the shedding of blood. These tragic realities are the consequence of a deviation from religious teachings. They result from a political manipulation of religions and from interpretations made by religious groups who, in the course of history, have taken advantage of the power of religious sentiment in the hearts of men and women in order to make them act in a way that has nothing to do with the truth of religion.

The Baha'i Writings identify the risk that a clash between mutually exclusive religious claims will pose a threat to peace. Here is 'Abdu'l-Bahá speaking a century ago:

> The chief cause [of the unrest among nations] is the misrepresentation of religion by the religious leaders and teachers. They teach their

> followers to believe that their own form of religion is the only one pleas-
> ing to God, and that followers of any other persuasion are condemned
> by the All-Loving Father and deprived of His Mercy and Grace. Hence
> arise among the peoples, disapproval, contempt, disputes and hatred.
> ('Abdu'l-Bahá, 1969, pp. 45–46)

The COVID-19 crisis sheds new light on the relationship between religious actors and public authorities. In the US, a number of figures on the so-called 'Christian right' have resisted public healthcare policies (Wilson, 2020). By contrast, the faith-in-action initiative promoted by Religions for Peace and UNICEF mentioned above calls on religious communities to cooperate with governments and other agencies in shaping and communicating policy. The 'lesson to be learned', perhaps, is that a multi-stakeholder dialogue can help religious communities to place their deepest values at the service of society.

When religion, political structures, and perceived group interests are confused and intermingled, misunderstanding thrives. Invitations to dialogue from public authorities can help enable religious communities to reflect on such difficulties. Sustained engagement can help the religions themselves to distinguish their permanent core values from attitudes and practices that relate only to a cultural context or that cannot easily be defended in a society oriented towards the interests of all. The frameworks of engagement that we have in mind, among their other benefits, can help us recover from the wrong turnings taken by religion.

MAP OF THIS BOOK

In this Introduction, we have discussed the present point of inflection in world history, the continuing influence of religious faith in global society, and the ways in which public authorities can usefully interact with a religious perspective. A *culture of encounter inclusive of the world's religious traditions* can become the catalyst for an enabling transformation in the sphere of multilateral diplomacy.

In an inherently pluralist world, how can the conversation about the future begin? Chapter 1 takes as its starting point the 'structural' questions asked by Socrates in another age of uncertainty. Comprehensive ethical frameworks are difficult to establish in the face of rapid change and the intermingling of cultures and traditions. Nevertheless, there is a read-across from one situation to another.

We can develop 'axioms of the historical imagination', founded on experience. These axioms, amounting to a form of historical and religious literacy, can interact with specialised competencies across all the relevant subject areas of multilateral diplomacy. In a pluralist global society, they can help us to embrace the commonality underlying our differences and to see ourselves, at some level, as companions on a shared journey.

Chapter 2 presents the first axiom: *we should examine the patterns of our behaviour in the light of all that we ought to know and can know.* The chapter offers a survey of diplomacy today and identifies the global phenomena that deserve urgent attention if we are to develop an approach to international relations that is fit-for-purpose.

Chapter 3 addresses the second axiom: *we should 'image' or visualise peace as the rightful possession of the human community as a whole.* The example of the 'Axial Age' suggests that civilisational values can change for the better and that such changes can be sustained over long periods.

Chapter 4 addresses the third axiom: *we should identify and explore the factors that accompany healing in a wounded social structure.* The chapter identifies ten such factors, or indicators – all typical of the religious perspective on human experience. We look on our ten themes as panels in a broad composition, in which separate images are interrelated and mutually supportive; the reader is invited into a 'conversation'.

Chapter 5 underlines the need for a paradigm shift in our understanding of effective action in international relations. Our fourth axiom is that *we should recognise that the starting position for political deliberation is inevitably non-ideal.* What cannot be pictured here and now, can become possible, given the right intermediate steps. Our fifth axiom is that *discernment in the midst of opacity in accordance with a common standard should become a core value in the conduct of international relations.* To follow the 'standard of justice', as opposed to the 'standard of self-interest', links one situation to another and is an act of shared hope. The chapter sketches, in conclusion, six dimensions of hope.

Chapter 6 addresses our sixth and final axiom: *we should give expression to a changing diplomatic culture through new frameworks of engagement.* Most states are committed, like the European Union, to 'a rules-based global order with multilateralism as its key principle and the UN at its core'. The chapter argues that to enable better diplomatic interaction, international organisations should use their convening power to bring about new, multilayered negotiating processes, inclusive of the representatives of religion. The chapter discusses the key parameters for consultations of this kind, the diplomatic 'product' that we should aim for, and the 'rules of engagement' for involving religions in transformational multilateral diplomacy.

The Epilogue illustrates our recommendations in a practical way. A brief outline is offered of what an all-European initiative might look like if, in the early 2020s, there were the political will to inaugurate a European regional process reflecting some of our ideas. Our argument does not stand or fall by this one example; other formats, other pathways, other geographical regions may prove more relevant in the long run to promoting the objectives of (i) new forms of diplomatic engagement inspired by religion and human values; (ii) forms of outreach whereby a deliberative assembly meets a high standard of 'accessibility'; and (iii) a step-change in region-to-region dialogue. In spanning cultural, religious, and political differences, an all-European conference can inspire parallel initiatives in neighbouring regions: the Mediterranean, Africa, the Middle East, the Silk Road, and East Asia.

NOTES

1 Bible translations are our own from the Septuaginta: revised edition, 2006, Deutsche Bibelgesellschaft, Stuttgart; and Novum Testamentum Graece et Latine, 11th edition, 1992, Rome: Pontificio Istituto Biblico.
2 In the speech 'Hope for this Hour', discussed in Mittleman (2009, p. 227).

REFERENCES

'Abdu'l-Bahá. (1969). *Paris Talks: Addresses Given by 'Abdu'l-Bahá in Paris in 1911* (11th ed.). London: Baha'i Publishing Trust.

'Abdu'l-Bahá. (1982). *Promulgation of Universal Peace: Talks Delivered by Abdu'l-Bahá during His Visit to the United States and Canada in 1912.* Compiled by Howard MacNutt (2nd ed.). Wilmette, IL: Baha'i Publishing Trust.

Aldred, J. (2019). *Licence to Be Bad: How Economics Corrupted Us.* London: Allen Lane.

Arendt, H. (1951). *The Origins of Totalitarianism*. New York: Schocken Books.

Bettiza, G. (2019). *Finding Faith in Foreign Policy: Religion and American Diplomacy in a Postsecular World*. Oxford and New York: Oxford University Press.

Collective Psychology Project (CPP). (2018). 'A Larger Us.' Project Launch Report. www.collectivepsychology.org

Council of the European Union. (2012). 'Treaty on the Functioning of the European Union (TFEU).' http://data.europa.eu/eli/treaty/tfeu_2012/oj

Davie, G., Ammerman, N.T., Huq, S., Leustean, L.N., Masoud, T., Moon, S., Olupona, J.K., Sinha, V., Smilde, D.A., Woodhead, L., Yang, F., and Zurlo, G. (2018). 'Religions and Social Progress: Critical Assessments and Creative Partnerships,' in *IPSP—International Panel on Social Progress, Rethinking Society for the 21st Century*, Volume 3: Transformations in Values, Norms, Cultures, pp. 641–676. Cambridge: Cambridge University Press. doi: https://doi.org/10.1017/9781108399661.003

Foroohar, R. (2019). *Don't Be Evil: The Case Against Big Tech*. London: Allen Lane.

Francis. (2015). '*Laudato Si: On Care for Our Common Home*.' [Encyclical letter]. Vatican City, Rome: Holy See Press office.

Ghosh, A. (2016). *The Great Derangement: Climate Change and the Unthinkable*. Chicago, IL and London: The University of Chicago Press.

Haass, R. (2017). *A World in Disarray: American Foreign Policy and the Crisis of the Old Order*. New York: Penguin Press.

Higher Committee of Human Fraternity (HCHF). (2019). 'Document on Human Fraternity and Living Together', signed by Pope Francis and Sheikh Ahmed el-Tayeb. www.forhumanfraternity.org and www.vatican.va

Hurrell, A. 2007. *On Global Order: Power, Values, and the Constitution of International Society*. New York: Oxford University Press.

International Covenant on Civil and Political Rights (ICCPR). (1976). Adopted and Opened for Signature, Ratification and Accession by General Assembly Resolution 2200A (XXI) of 16 December 1966; entered into force 23 March 1976, in accordance with Article 49. Viewed from www.ohchr.org

Johnston, D. (ed.). (2003). *Faith-Based Diplomacy: Trumping Realpolitik*. New York: Oxford University Press.

Joint Learning Initiative on Faith & Local Communities. (2020). 'Launch of Global Multi-Religious Faith-in-Action COVID-19 Initiative.' https://jliflc.com

Lessenich, S. (2019). *Living Well at Others' Expense: The Hidden Costs of Western Prosperity*. Cambridge: Polity Press (German edition, 2016).

Lane, M. (2014). *Greek and Roman Political Ideas*. London: Pelican.

Levitsky, S., and Ziblatt, D. (2018). *How Democracies Die: What History Reveals about Our Future*. New York: Penguin Random House.

Macron, E. (2018). *Discours du Président de la République, Emmanuel Macron, à la Conférence des évêques de France au Collège des Bernardins*, Collège des Bernardins, Paris, 9 April 2018.

Marrou, H.-I. (1958) *Saint Augustin et la Fin de la Culture Antique*. Paris: Editions De Boccard.

Mittleman, A. (2009). *Hope in a Democratic Age: Philosophy, Religion, and Political Theory*. Oxford: Oxford University Press.

Ochs, P. (2019). *Religion without Violence: The Practice and Philosophy of Scriptural Reasoning*. Eugene, OR: Cascade Books.

Organisation for Security and Cooperation in Europe (OSCE). (2003). 'Strategy Document for the Economic and Environmental Dimension.' www.osce.org

Organisation for Security and Cooperation in Europe (OSCE). (2013). 'Ministerial Council Decision No. 3/13: Freedom, Conscience, Religion or Belief.' http://hdl.handle.net/20.500.12389/21735

Organisation for Security and Cooperation in Europe (OSCE), Office for Democratic Institutions and Human Rights (ODIHR)/Venice Commission. (2014). *Guidelines on the Legal Personality of Religious or Belief Communities*. Warsaw: ODIHR.

Organisation for Security and Cooperation in Europe (OSCE), Office for Democratic Institutions and Human Rights (ODIHR). (2019). *Freedom of Religion or Belief and Security: Policy Guidance*. Warsaw: ODIHR.

Pettit, P. (2014). *Just Freedom: A Moral Compass for a Complex World*. New York: Norton.

Pew Research Center. (2015). 'The Future of World Religions: Population Growth Projections, 2010–2050.' www.pewresearch.org

Thapar, V. (2020). 'Press Restart: A Moment of Rebuilding Is on Us. Best Minds Must Contribute', Indian Express, 13 April 2020. https://indianexpress.com/article/opinion/columns/coronavirus-pandemic-climate-change-agreements-environmental-disaster-china-virus-6359507/

United Nations Environment Programme (UNEP). 2020. 'Faith for Earth Initiative.' www.un-environment.org/about-un-environment/faith-earth-initiative

Wilson, J. (2020). 'The Right Wing Christian Preachers in Deep Denial over Covid-19's Danger,' *Guardian*, 4 April. www.theguardian.com/us-news/2020/apr/04/America-rightwing-christian-preachers-virus-hoax

STRUCTURAL QUESTIONS IN 21ST-CENTURY DIPLOMACY

PUBLIC TRUTH IN A PLURALIST GLOBAL SOCIETY

Gandhi promoted the production of *khadi*, hand-spun cotton yarn, as the symbol and spearhead of an inclusive, non-violent social and economic order based on useful work. *Swaraj* of the least powerful – the self-determination of the poor – became the touchstone, or talisman, of political progress: 'to a people famishing and idle, the only acceptable form in which God can dare appear is work and the promise of food as wages' (Gandhi, 2006, p. 257).

Gandhi's option for the poor, though often criticised for a lack of policy detail, is reflected in the SDGs in the formulations: 'no one should be left behind' and 'reaching the last first'. 'The poorest and those most in need' are central to the Document on Human Fraternity signed by Pope Francis and Grand Imam Ahmed el-Tayeb (HCHF, 2019).

The axioms that we propose in this book function like Gandhi's talisman as a common criterion of evaluation in a variety of circumstances. Our aim is to promote a diplomatic practice in which guiding values, understood in a new way, as 'transcripts from life' (Radhakrishnan, 1980 [1927], p. 14), interact effectively with specialised competencies across all the relevant subject areas of multilateral diplomacy.

In anthropological or civilisational terms, our most urgent task is to affirm *the possibility of an effective public truth*. In a pluralist global society, we need to embrace the commonality underlying our differences (important and inevitable as these differences are); to frame our differences in such a way that we continue to understand one another; and to see ourselves at some level as companions on a shared journey.

Against this background, our thesis is that well-designed 'frameworks of engagement' can narrow 'the gap between global problems and our capacity to meet them' (Haass, 2020, p. 3). By creating such frameworks, we would signal our openness to new designs for living.

The expectancy that inspires this book is that if the engagement of public authorities with religious traditions becomes our compass, the global political journey will veer in the coming decades towards the 'true north' of solidarity, sharing, stewardship of the planet, and *swaraj* for the most vulnerable – and will do this palpably, in ways that people will find compelling in terms of their lived experience.

FINDING A COMMON LANGUAGE

Religions, on entering the public square, become part of a wider dialogue or conversation. They need to make themselves understood in the common language of reason. A contemporary authority on the Chinese tradition asks whether Confucianism can contribute over the coming decades to a 'more mature' way of thinking about international political issues. For this to happen, he argues, Chinese thinkers will need to 'justify Confucian values in terms that do not require prior acceptance of Confucianism' (Chan, 2014, p. 23). This is exactly the spirit of the dialogue we recommend in this book. None of us can expect everyone else to embrace our own worldview as the price of entering the conversation.

HOW THEN, IN AN INHERENTLY PLURALIST WORLD, CAN THE CONVERSATION ABOUT THE FUTURE BEGIN?

In Athens in the 5th century BCE, an 'inherited conglomerate' of ideas (Dodds, 1951), including a mythological account of the gods, was no longer persuasive, at least for many people. In philosophy, history, ethnography, medical research, and the theatre, as well as in political practice, new ideas were tested. Socrates is the emblematic figure in this transition (Canto-Sperber, 2000; Sassi, 2018). Earlier philosophers are classified as the 'pre-Socratics'; later schools of philosophy refer back to Socrates.

Socrates and his contemporaries approach the question of values in politics in a disinterested spirit of enquiry, returning to basic 'structural' questions in a manner that sets an example for today's global situation in which no single vision of the truth prevails. The basic 'Socratic question' – *how should we live?*, or *what is our design for living?* – comes first. The structural questions listed below emanate from this initial question.

> If every action aims at some good, is there a higher good, such as happiness, which is valued for its own sake and becomes the 'unifying focus of all our scattered enterprises'?
>
> (Veale, 2006, p. 238)

> Which avenues of enquiry are relevant to politics? Are there forms of knowledge, such as (in ancient Greece) medical expertise or ship-building, that are valid in themselves, irrespective of anyone's overall worldview? In our search for a 'unifying focus', is there a role for 'wisdom' or the 'wise person' – poet, prophet, or philosopher – who relies on something more than problem-solving investigations within a delimited field of enquiry? How does a political dispensation based on coercion become a dispensation based on freely given consent? Are we prepared to suffer for the sake of others? Is there a common life or collective well-being that is more than the sum of our private interests? Should the state help people to become good, or to pursue 'the good life', through law, education, ceremony, public spending? Who has a share in the common life? Do we need communities distinct from the political community? How should these communities intersect with the political community? How should different political communities relate to one another?

In the 21st century, even more than in the past, comprehensive ethical frameworks are difficult to establish in the face of rapid change and the intermingling of cultures and traditions. Nevertheless, there is a read-across from one political situation to another, and from one cultural context to another. Because of this, we can develop 'axioms of the historical imagination', with a view to radical, practical, and inclusive action:

- *radical*, because of the scale of the challenge
- *practical*, because of the difference between *action with interpretation* and a mere system of ideas – 'what is written [engraved on stone] kills, the Spirit gives life' (St. Paul, 2 Corinthians 3:6–7; Lash, 1981, p. 285)
- *inclusive*, because each tradition needs to work with others for the sake of the future

On all sides, we need to go deep enough in exploring our assumptions to uncover the 'lateral roots' and unspoken commonalities that can bind one cultural tradition to another. We need to recognise, in a 'performative' way, that we share, and depend on, a single, small planet in danger. All individuals and peoples should have access to what they need in order to live.

THE SEARCH FOR COMMON VALUES

In terms of the search for common ground at the global level, one of the most significant developments of recent years is concerned directly with religion, namely the rapprochement between the Holy See and China, announced in September 2018 (Spadaro, 2018). The dialogue between the Holy See and China is focused, for now, on the procedures for appointing bishops. This is a question at the intersection of freedom of religion with public policy. However, a broader dialogue on global issues, embracing other actors as well, is to be expected in due course (Narvaja, 2017).

The structural questions about life in community faced by the Greeks of the 5th century BCE are similar to the structural questions raised in the tradition of thought in which Confucius is the leading figure. Central to this similarity is the integration of ethics and politics. Once we accept that the goal of political organisation is to underpin a design for living, we are drawn to further questions about the purposes and responsibilities of human life. Above all, we see the imperfection of our political and economic systems in the light of our ideals. For those of us educated in the traditions of the European Enlightenment, reappropriating the deep resources of our own tradition, which did not always happen during the

18th century, can help us prepare for a global conversation inclusive of the increasingly important Chinese/Confucian perspective.

At 'ground level', indigenous peoples have always understood that ethics and politics are aspects of the same question. 'Ordinary people' have a sense of fairness or unfairness, of justice or the corruption of justice. They understand very well the read-across from one people's experience to another's:

'*Cad a dhéanfaimid feasta gan adhmad?*' (What shall we do from now on without timber?)

This 18th-century Irish lament for the destruction of trees could be sung with equal passion in the 21st century in Rajasthan or on the banks of the Amazon. A people grieving over the destruction of their forest or their fisheries, a mother mourning over a conscript son killed in battle – no moral philosophy can tell them they are 'wrong'. In China, Mencius tells the parable about villagers who rescue a child from drowning; the point being that the instinct of solidarity is innate at the base of society. In the round, human experience poses a strong challenge to the hypothesis that we are 'self-made gods with only the laws of physics to keep us company' (Harari, 2014, p. 415).

Today, the main cultural traditions of humanity, including the world religions, are seen to have many important values in common. Another development of global significance, the engagement of Christian theologians with the Hindu tradition, was taken further than ever before by the work of the Jesuits in India in the late 20th century (Dupuis, 1999). Some religious leaders are beginning to ask whether the diversity of religion or belief is providential. Here, once again, are Pope Francis and Grand Imam Ahmed el-Tayeb, speaking with one voice (HCHF, 2019): 'The pluralism and diversity of religions … are willed by God in His wisdom, through which He created human beings'.

To identify common elements at the roots of European and Chinese civilisations is an act of intellectual consolidation that can be helpful not only for a future dialogue between Europe (in the broad sense) and China, but for other new and inclusive modes of dialogue at the global level, and in particular, for the dialogue between public authorities and religious communities.

The challenge for the religions is to understand the unanswered questions that arise in all cultures, including the sense that we live in the shadow of terrible injustice and that our life's journey is towards an unseen destination. At their best, the religions can change the focus of our attention and bring healing, consolation, and hope to our wounded social structures; but they do not reinvent the 'social question'.

Today, Chinese scholars are actively exploring their own rich traditions in the light of current challenges. There is a vivid debate in India going to the roots of India's varied civilisation. In liberal democracies, the gains we have made in such areas as free speech and the separation of powers will be more secure if they can be shown to serve a broad, 'Socratic' or 'Confucian' conception of the common good. In the words of the contemporary Chinese scholar already quoted above, 'the language of virtue, responsibility, and benevolent care' can enrich the 'modern language of freedom, rights, and democracy' (Chan, 2014, p. xiv). In 2020, the year of the coronavirus, who can doubt the wisdom of this judgement?

THE DANGER OF FUNDAMENTALISM

At this point in the argument, we open a parenthesis concerning fundamentalism in religion, by which we mean a failure to 'process' ancient texts within living communities open to the different forms of knowledge.

In taking up the challenge posed by Socrates, we do not have a falsely idealistic picture of ancient civilisations. On the contrary, steep social hierarchies, doctrines regarding the inferiority of some groups, and the idea that organisation for warfare is the cornerstone of a successful society are never shaken off in the ancient world. Within this web of beliefs, the institution of slavery works its way to the very centre, as we see in Plato (a societal elite focused on a virtue located in the individual soul) and Aristotle (the 'natural slave').

Genesis, Exodus, Numbers, Deuteronomy, and other biblical texts reveal, no less than other ancient civilisations, an impoverished political imagination:

> I will send my terror in front of you ... I will send the pestilence[1] in front of you, which shall drive out the Hivites, the Canaanites, and the Jebusites.
>
> (Exodus 23:27–28)

> The slaves that you have, men and women, shall come from the nations round you; from these you may purchase slaves, men and women.

You may also purchase them from the children of the strangers who live among you, and from the families living with you who have been born on your soil. They shall be your property.

(Leviticus 25:44–45)

Kill all the male children. Kill also all the women who have slept with a man. Spare only the lives of the young girls who have not slept with a man *and take them for yourselves.*

(Numbers 31:17–19, emphasis added)

But as for the towns of these peoples that Yahweh your God is giving you as an inheritance, you must not let anything that breathes remain alive. You shall annihilate them.

(Deuteronomy 20:15–17)

These biblical texts, and others like them, have not been quietly forgotten over the centuries; on the contrary, they have been deployed repeatedly in defence of barbaric actions, often in connection with European colonisation (Prior, 1997).

What Rajmohan Gandhi (1999, p. 35) states of the Mahabharata is relevant to many sacred texts:

Not only must we, with all hands, grasp this great book – this powerful vehicle careering down the slope of India's history; we must stop it in its tracks, and control and use it for India's peace and joy.

One of the most important strategies for dealing with the 'out-of-control vehicle', or any other dangerous web of beliefs, is to subject them to close examination in the light of every form of knowledge available to us – always remembering Cicero's injunction (*De Officiis*, III 19): 'Is it not a shame that philosophers should be in doubt regarding moral issues on which ordinary people (*rustici*) have no doubts at all?'[2]

CONVERGENCES IN CONTEMPORARY THOUGHT

No political model, school of theology, or academic discipline, taken in isolation, can provide the moral resources to restore meaning to the public debate on foreign policy and international relations. At the same time, the transformation that we are looking for will not arise in an intellectual context lacking in structure and definition.

What is to be done? In his speech on receiving the Charlemagne Prize in 2016, Pope Francis advocated new forms of coalition – 'cultural, educational, philosophical, and religious'. We accept this as a fair description of the way forward. In the interests of 'situational awareness', we will do our best in the next few paragraphs to take encouragement from recent or contemporary thinkers in a number of areas.

Creative literature has always been a prism through which to interpret political situations. In fiction and in the theatre, a believable narrative has truth value. Samuel Beckett (2010) and others explore what it means to be together here and now, in communion with one another, even as narratives break down. Poetry has its own truth value. In an essay of 1913, Osip Mandelstam states, 'A work of art attracts the great majority only insofar as it illuminates the artist's world view ... the consciousness of our rightness is dearer to us than anything else in poetry' (in Harris, 1991, pp. 61–62). Socrates, in his death cell, was uncertain whether poetry or philosophy better serves humanity's quest for meaning (Plato, *Phaedo*, 1914, pp. 60–61).

Wittgenstein's private language argument, Buber's *I and Thou*, and Levinas's focus on intersubjective responsibility have profound implications for political philosophy – and ultimately for our understanding of human evolution and identity. The culture of encounter that we propose in this book can draw inspiration from these thinkers and, in general, from the major questions of 20th-century philosophy (MacIntyre, 1988): does being a person imply 'relationality'? Do ethics depend on shared meaning within a tradition? Should we in some circumstances hold back from conceptualisation in order to avoid a too hasty synthesis?

In economics, a range of contemporary work converges with the ethical and cultural agenda suggested in this book. We think, for example, of writers who challenge 'shareholder value' as the ultimate measure of a company's performance (Galbraith and now very many others, including the US Business Roundtable and the signatories of the Davos Manifesto of January 2020); who question the explanatory power of an economic model based on isolated choice-making individuals; who map the social consequences, hidden structures (Lessenich, 2019), and relentless advance (Piketty, 2014) of inequality; who analyse the unintended consequences of 'technical' decisions taken by central bankers (Tucker, 2018); or who argue that competition policy is failing in practice to achieve its own stated purpose of restraining the dominance of the largest companies. Recently, E. Glen Weyl, the leader of the new on-line movement RadicalxChange, argues in his manifesto that capitalism as currently conceived, based on private ownership on a gigantic scale, is in conflict with the collective nature of value creation in a modern economy (Weyl, 2019, pp. 4–5).

In due course, economic theory will have to take account of government interventions during the coronavirus crisis. In many cases, these interventions appear to go against economic 'orthodoxy', in relation, for example, to market distortion, the role played by incentives, the risk of inflation, and the use of 'GDP' as the sole measure of economically relevant activity.

The Collective Psychology Project (CPP), already cited, traces the connection between our inner, psychological lives on the one hand, and 'real world' factors on the other – much as economists are learning to map the changing ethical assumptions associated, in practice, with the rise and fall of certain economic models (Aldred, 2019).

The insights of the natural sciences and the conduct of scientific investigation are central to all efforts to find a common path for humanity in the 21st century. We rely, most obviously, on those who shape the debate on climate change and lead the search for the vaccines and screening techniques that can help restrain pandemics.

In the sphere of historical investigation, we compare our approach with that of scholars of civilisations and the 'lateral roots' that may or may not connect them. We accept that civilisations follow a trajectory in which there are pivotal phases. Aristotle observes that historical changes can occur within a time scale that falls outside the usual scope of political analysis; for example, the changes brought about by successful water management in the Nile Delta over many generations. There is a point of contact between Aristotle's thinking on long-term environmental factors in historical causation and the recent concept that the 'terrestrial' has become a political actor (Latour, 2018).

For students of world order, a key question is whether, in practice, the most consequential issues are addressed (Hurrell, 2007; Kissinger, 2014; Pettit, 2014; Haass, 2017; Lessenich, 2019). 'Realism', as a value in foreign policy and international relations, should refer in the first instance to *contact with reality*. Is it 'realistic', in describing value creation in the economy, to ignore important contributory factors? Is it 'realistic', in foreign policy, to pretend that moral principles that influence conduct are not 'real'?

FREEDOM AND TRUTH

As a young person gradually assumes personal responsibility, he or she internalises the values of parents and teachers and acts (paradoxically, some would say) in greater freedom. Similarly, in a well-governed society, citizens assent freely to laws, regulations, and day-to-day decisions, and act according to a logic of solidarity, even when the law is weak or unclear. Good government inspires personal, psychological, and political maturity. The quality of our relationships is always at stake.

Every society has rules; where the rules fit together and make a reasonable claim on our conscience, we speak of justice or just laws. Justice is objective in a way that charity or philanthropy is not; it concerns the rights or entitlements of the parties. The 'justice' that holds human society together is an accessible truth, capable of improvement and adaptation.

The creative exercise of freedom is the foundation of a society based on relationships of trust. To be enjoyed in any deep sense, freedom requires capabilities and resources; the social stability and general well-being that predispose many of us to obey the law are not evenly distributed in society, as we see in the sprawling prisons of the US. We know that superficially similar forms of government can give rise to very different outcomes in terms of the prevailing ethos and atmosphere. Inner circles and corrupt practices can arise in any society; they can arise simultaneously in different societies, as if by contagion. In this perspective, many political thinkers are more concerned with character, with how people look at the world, than with constitutional forms.

In today's global society, there is scope for nation states to reshape their foreign policy goals and contribute to the development of a multifaceted global culture supportive of all individuals and all peoples and capable of meeting with general acceptance (cf. Halle, 1952). A key obstacle to a project of this kind is that in recent decades the politics of creative solidarity has been under challenge from dominant orthodoxies that, in extolling freedom, attach little weight to personal maturity, the capabilities on which the exercise of freedom depends, or the quality of relationships. A case is made that diplomacy is merely the management of the brutal politics of power and that the 'market', understood as an entrenched, impersonal system, is a fundamental good.

For such thinkers, international law, if considered at all, has little density or content. For example, a prominent American thinker, in an influential and well-reviewed work, claims that 'war is a creative activity of civilised man' (Bobbitt, 2002, p. xxxi). In the light of this thesis, he argues that the UN Charter is not credible, and the global future will be determined by nation states that secure a popular mandate for the pursuit of military ascendancy with a view to controlling markets. Another well-known US commentator argues, more simply, that 'leadership demands a pagan ethos' (Kaplan, 2002). According to authors like these, international relations are never directed, in 'reality', to an ethical and social end; on the contrary, outcomes are determined by powerful actors advancing their selfish interests.

A variant of this bleak understanding of social relations is that 'market' is a univocal term denoting a fundamental good, and that the functioning of the market must be protected against questioning and interference. The Chicago school of economics, focusing on a supposedly scientific 'description' of the economy, and elevating the role of self-interest, has points in common with the 'realist' school in international relations.

A binary model of market–plus–state (selfishness in the market, duty to the state) leaves many transactions to unfold outside any recognisable ethical framework. Individuals are led to believe that significant actions are 'negligible' with respect to social outcomes (Lane, 2012, pp. 52–65). Public authorities are unable to keep track of important developments. It has even been argued that a culture of impunity and 'moral hazard' is built into the very concept of a limited company:

> Our limited liability in that Société Anonyme called the world makes each of us disclaim personal responsibility for any crime incurred by the Joint-Stock Company as a whole.
>
> (Gerhardie, 1981, p. 312)

Richard Haass, a moderate and mainstream US commentator who has served in government, makes a severe judgement on the quality of relationships in US society and the consequences of this for foreign policy:

> Long before COVID-19 ravaged the earth, there had already been a precipitous decline in the appeal of the American model. Thanks to

> persistent political gridlock, gun violence, the mismanagement that led to the 2008 global financial crisis, the opioid epidemic, and more, what America represented grew increasingly unattractive to many. The federal government's slow, incoherent, and all too often ineffective response to the pandemic will reinforce the already widespread view that the United States has lost its way.

(Haass, 2020, p. 2)

The road to a restoration of faith in democracy passes through a richer understanding of the meaning of freedom.

TOWARDS A BROAD UNDERSTANDING OF REASON

In international relations theory, the 'principle of diffuse reciprocity' implies that if everyone follows the agreed rules, everyone will benefit significantly over time. In diplomacy conceived in this way, what is 'real' is in part a reflection of our values and how we are persuaded to act. The 'descriptive' and the 'prescriptive' are not completely separable.

A hard-edged 'realism' in international relations, or a conception of the economy founded only on individual 'choice' within an impersonal market, does not pass the test of contact with reality. The 'science' of those who use only the methods of the laboratory to understand human society amounts to a self-imposed narrowing of the scope of reason. Even then, their scientific model may fall short of how physicists and biologists understand the investigation of nature. We are never mere observers; it has been said that 'the result of the experiment, nature's answer, depends on the question put to it' (Ratzinger, 2004, p. 175).

In the ancient Greek tradition, the Muses inspire endeavour in all the departments of knowledge, from mathematics and music to poetry and the work of justice. They are the daughters of Zeus and Memory, of a providential god and the human hunger for meaning. In the *Theogony* (700 BCE), Hesiod describes a certain kind of judge, touched by the Muses, who 'can put a quick and expert end even to a great quarrel' (Lattimore, 1959, p. 128). When the people go astray, a political leader blessed with the gift of the Muses guides them with gentle arguments. In other words, there is a close kinship between intellectual creativity and public reasoning.

'We know how to say many false things that seem like true sayings', sing the Muses in the passage we are quoting. For Hesiod, our subjectivity, our seeming awareness of being in possession of the truth, is capable of being deceived; a poem or a prophetic claim must be checked against criteria that we find in other parts of our lives. In the Hindu tradition, insight into the nature of reality (*darśana*) is a response of the whole personality; the religious seer 'is compelled to justify his inmost convictions in a way that satisfies the thought of the age' (Radhakrishnan, 1980 [1927], p. 14).

In personifying the source of truth, and claiming a personal relationship with that source, Hesiod establishes freedom of conscience and the possibility of creative action. In then directing his attention outwards, towards the society that he seeks to influence through his poetry, Hesiod accepts the discipline of public discourse. The receptivity of the artist accompanies the search for explanation and accountability in the community.

There is a line of continuity, stretching across 1,200 years of classical civilisation, from Hesiod on Mount Helicon to the Christian martyr Boethius in his cell in Pavia in the early 6th century (cf. Marrou, 1956). Boethius, aware that his readership includes many who are not Christians and that Christians are divided among themselves, presents his last testament as a revelation of the lady 'Philosophy', who appears at his bedside and gathers her dress into a fold to dry his weeping eyes: 'when Socrates had his victory over an unjust death, was I not there by his side?' (*The Consolation of Philosophy*, I, 3). In a playful passage, 'Lady Philosophy' takes over the care of the patient Boethius from the Muses of Mount Helikon. But she, no less than they, is happy to speak in verse.

Dante was inspired by Boethius. Fundamental to Dante's thought is that intelligence – the *luce intellettual, piena d'amore* ('the light of intellect that is full of love') (Dante, 1978, Canto XXX) – reaches towards forms of understanding that lie beyond what we can measure in the material universe. Dante's 'Muse' is a loved person – Beatrice.

Percy Bysshe Shelley wrote his 'Defence of Poetry' as a response to social injustice in the Industrial Revolution. For Shelley, who did not describe himself as a religious man, 'the most unfailing herald, companion, and follower of the awakening of a great people to work a beneficial change … is Poetry'. There is a natural correlation between poetry and 'beneficial change' because the work of the poet – 'poetry in a restricted sense' – 'has a common source with all other forms of order and beauty' (Shelley, 2003, p. 700).

In Shelley's vision, poetry is moral, not because it offers a political platform, or role models of good behaviour, or because the poet himself is a role model, but because the perspective of the poet – his impartial care for the truth of situations – reaches towards goodness.

In the Western tradition, a central philosophical debate is expressed in the distinction between 'faith' and 'reason', '*fides*' and '*ratio*'. *Fides* is often thought of as subjective and *ratio* as objective. But this is an artificial distinction. Hesiod, as we have seen, tests the promptings of the Muses against political criteria. To 'credit poetry', in Seamus Heaney's phrase, is very often to accept the claims of a public truth; Heaney cites the truth-telling role of the Russian poets Anna Akhmatova and Osip Mandelstam (Heaney, 1995). A personal commitment to values that can be shared with others is well translated by the Latin *fides*; in this important word, the ideas of 'faith', 'hope', 'trust', and 'personal commitment' resonate together.

We can envisage a new distinction. On the one hand stands *fides*, meaning faith, hope, and personal commitment, and on the other hand stands *passio*, meaning subjective emotion or feeling. *Passio* is *passive*, in the literal sense, and is easily divorced from good judgement. *Fides* is anchored in the public realm in which reason plays its part.

Shakespeare's Ophelia is broken by her circumstances:

> Poor Ophelia,
> Divided from herself and her fair judgment.
> > (Shakespeare, 1968, Act 4, Scene 5, lines 83–84)

Hamlet, unlike Ophelia, knows what it means to make practical decisions, as he explains to Horatio:

> Give me that man
> That is not passion's slave, and I will wear him
> In my heart's core.
> > (Act 3, Scene 2, lines 69–71)

Hamlet also recovers hope:

> There's a divinity that shapes our ends,
> Rough-hew them how we will.
> > (Act 5, Scene 2, lines 10–11)

The courage of the rightful Prince of Denmark, rooted in both *ratio* and *fides*, restores order to his country at the price of his own life.

Grappling, each in their own way, with a broad understanding of reason, Hesiod, Boethius, Dante, Shakespeare, and Shelley fit easily into the dialogue of cultures that today's world so badly needs. Some children of the Western Enlightenment are inclined to manhandle the Muses. In the dialogue of cultures, they will be seen by many of their interlocutors as operating within a local, limited perspective.

NOTES

1 Literally, 'hornets': the precise interpretation of this phrase is disputed; the passage as a whole describes the step-by-step disabling and destruction of the societies in question.

2 The *De Officiis*, 'On Duties', composed in dangerous circumstances not long before Cicero's murder, became one of the most influential classical texts. In the 4th century, St. Ambrose set out his ethical vision under the title *De Officiis*, echoing Cicero and implicitly comparing and contrasting secular and Judaeo-Christian values. The 'just war' tradition in the West has its roots in St. Augustine's reading of Cicero's *De Officiis*.

REFERENCES

Aldred, J. (2019). *Licence to Be Bad: How Economics Corrupted Us*. London: Allen Lane.

Beckett, S. (2010). *Waiting for Godot: A Tragicomedy in Two Acts*. London: Faber and Faber (first published in Paris in 1952 as *En attendant Godot*).

Bobbitt, P. (2002). *The Shield of Achilles: War, Peace, and the Course of History*. New York: Allen Lane.

Boethius. (1918). *The Theological Tractates and Consolation of Philosophy*, translated and edited by H.F. Stewart, E.K. Rand, and S.J. Tester. Loeb Classical Library. Cambridge: Harvard University Press.

Canto-Sperber, M. (2000). 'Socrates,' in J. Brunschwig and G.E.R. Lloyd (eds.), *A Guide to Greek Thought: Major Figures and Trends*, pp. 223–240. Cambridge, MA: Belknap Press (French edition, 1997).

Chan, J. (2014). *Confucian Perfectionism: A Political Philosophy for Modern Times*. Princeton and Oxford: Princeton University Press.

Cicero. (1913). *De Officiis*, translated by W. Miller. Loeb Classical Library. Cambridge: Harvard University Press.

Collective Psychology Project (CPP). (2018). 'A Larger Us.' Project launch report. www.collectivepsychology.org

Dante. (1978). '*Paradiso*, Canto XXX,' in P. Milano (ed.), *The Portable Dante*. London: Penguin.

Dodds, E.R. (1951). *The Greeks and the Irrational*. Berkeley, Los Angeles, London: University of California Press.

Dupuis, J. (1999). *Toward a Christian Theology of Religious Pluralism*. New York: Orbis Books.

Francis. (2016). *Conferral of the Charlemagne Prize: Address of His Holiness Pope Francis*, May 6, Vatican. www.vatican.va

Gandhi, R. (1999). *Revenge and Reconciliation: Understanding South Asian History*. New Delhi: Penguin Books India.

Gandhi, R. (2006). *Mohandas: A True Story of a Man, His People, and an Empire*. New Delhi: Penguin Books India.

Gerhardie, W. (1981). *God's Fifth Column: A Biography of the Age 1890–1940*. New York: Simon and Schuster.

Haass, R. (2017). *A World in Disarray: American Foreign Policy and the Crisis of the Old Order*. New York: Penguin Press.

Haass, R. (2020). 'The Pandemic Will Accelerate History Rather than Reshape It: Not Every Crisis Is a Turning Point,' *Foreign Affairs*, April 7, 2020. www. foreignaffairs.com/articles/united-states/2020-04-07/pandemic-will-accelerate-history-rather-reshape-it

Halle, L.J. (1952). *Civilization and Foreign Policy: An Inquiry for Americans*. New York: Harper.

Harari, J.N. (2014). *Sapiens: A Brief History of Humankind*. London: Harvill Secker.

Harris, J.G. (ed.). (1991). *Osip Mandelstam: The Collected Critical Prose and Letters*, translated by J.G. Harris and C. Link. London: Collins Harvill.

Heaney, S. (1995). *Crediting Poetry: The Nobel Lecture*. Oldcastle: The Gallery Press.

Higher Committee of Human Fraternity (HCHF). (2019). 'Document on Human Fraternity and Living Together,' signed by Pope Francis and Sheikh Ahmed el-Tayeb. www.forhumanfraternity.org and www.vatican.va

Hurrell, A. (2007). *On Global Order: Power, Values, and the Constitution of International Society*. New York: Oxford University Press.

Kaplan, R.D. (2002). *Warrior Politics: Why Leadership Demands a Pagan Ethos*. New York: Random House.

Kissinger, H. (2014). *World Order: Reflections on the Character of Nations and the Course of History*. London: Allen Lane.

Lane, M. (2012). *Eco-Republic: What the Ancients Can Teach Us about Ethics, Virtue, and Sustainable Living*. Princeton: Princeton University Press.

Lash, N. (1981). *A Matter of Hope: A Theologian's Reflections on the Thought of Karl Marx*. London: Darton, Longman, and Todd.

Latour, B. (2018). *Down to Earth: Politics in the New Climatic Regime*. Cambridge: Polity Press (French edition, 2017).

Lattimore, R. (translator). (1959). *Hesiod*. Ann Arbor: University of Michigan Press.

Lessenich, S. (2019). *Living Well at Others' Expense: The Hidden Costs of Western Prosperity*. Cambridge: Polity Press (German edition, 2016).

MacIntyre, A.C. (1988). *Whose Justice? Which Rationality?* London: Duckworth.

Marrou, H.I. (1956). *A History of Education in Antiquity*. New York: Sheed and Ward.

Narvaja, J.L. (2017). 'Il Significato della Politica Internazionale di Francesco,' *La Civiltà Cattolica* 4009, III, pp. 8–15.

Pettit, P. (2014). *Just Freedom: A Moral Compass for a Complex World*. New York: Norton.

Piketty, T. (2014). *Capital in the Twenty-First Century*. (French edition published 2013 as *Le capital au XXI siècle*, Editions du Seuil). Cambridge, MA: Belknap Press.

Plato. (1914). *Plato: Euthyphro, Apology, Crito, Phaedo, Phaedrus*, edited and translated by H.N. Fowler. Loeb Classical Library. Cambridge: Harvard University Press.

Prior, M. (1997). *The Bible and Colonialism: A Moral Critique*. Sheffield: Sheffield Academic Press.

Radhakrishnan, S. (1980). *The Hindu View of Life*. London: Unwin Paperbacks (first published in 1927).

Ratzinger, J. (2004). *Introduction to Christianity*, translated by J.R. Foster, (rev. ed.). San Francisco: Ignatius Press (first published in 1968).

Sassi, M.M. (2018). *The Beginnings of Philosophy in Greece*. Princeton: Princeton University Press.

Shakespeare, W. (1968). *The Tragedy of Hamlet, Prince of Denmark* (J.D. Wilson, ed.). Cambridge: Cambridge University Press.

Shelley, P. (2003). 'A Defence of Poetry,' in Z. Leader and M. O'Neill (eds.), *Percy Bysshe Shelley: The Major Works*, pp. 674–701. Oxford: Oxford University Press.

Spadaro, A. (2018). 'L'Accordo tra Cina e Santa Sede,' *La Civiltà Cattolica* 4039, pp. 8–21.

Tucker, P. (2018). *Unelected Power: The Quest for Legitimacy in Central Banking and the Regulatory State*. Princeton: Princeton University Press.

Veale, J. (2006). *Manifold Gifts: Ignatian Essays on Spirituality*. Oxford: Way Books.

Weyl, E.G. (2019). 'The Political Philosophy of RadicalxChange.' www.radicalxchange.org/blog/posts/2019-12-30

KNOWING WHAT WE OUGHT TO KNOW

THE ISSUES THAT FACE 21ST-CENTURY DIPLOMACY

KNOWING WHAT WE OUGHT TO KNOW AND CAN KNOW

Our thesis is that a global culture of encounter and dialogue inclusive of religious traditions, promoted and facilitated by international organisations, and encouraged by governments, can lead to a measure of consensus based on six axioms that together amount to a liberating form of historical and religious literacy. Our first axiom is that we need to *examine the patterns of our behaviour in the light of all that we ought to know and can know.* At issue is the range and character of the knowledge on which political deliberation rests.

Decision making requires knowledge of the facts. In ancient Greece, it was said that the Athenians made the disastrous decision to invade Sicily, 'most of them not knowing the size of the island or the number of its inhabitants' (Thucydides, 1996, VI.1). There are many 21st-century equivalents of such culpable blindness. Denying that climate change poses a serious danger or insisting that market forces alone can correct problems in the digital world are obvious examples.

In relation to our *obligation to know*, there is more at stake than a willingness to look at evidence, important as that is. Equally important is our willingness to create the conditions for learning, and the vantage point from which we examine the evidence. Our self-understanding, our historical perspective, our current priorities, and our receptivity to other points of view all come into play.

Very often our interpretation of evidence is compromised at root level by presuppositions or assumptions that remain hidden, even from ourselves. The key principle at stake is whether subjective good faith, even if shared within a group, in itself justifies our actions. We see the problem clearly in such extreme cases as the Waffen-SS, which appears to have enjoyed high morale in the midst of atrocious evil-doing.

Ignoring, despising, or undervaluing the sufferings of others is not something that happens only rarely. On many issues, we citizens prefer not to know everything that is going on, or not to bring our awareness into focus. In W. H. Auden's (1976, p. 179) poem, 'Musée des Beaux Arts', one person's disaster is for others 'not an important failure'. Historians recognise that the 'official' narrative of events may obscure important aspects of what really happened; that is why the new museum of the American Revolution in Philadelphia tells the history of the Revolution through the eyes of the British, the American colonists, the French, the African Americans, and the indigenous people.

A much-respected commentator of our own day, Yuval Noah Harari (2018, p. 226), observes that our chosen standpoint may ultimately mislead us: 'Most of the injustices in the contemporary world result from large-scale structural biases rather than from individual prejudices.'

In this chapter, we explore our first axiom concerning the obligation to know by means of a short survey of global realities. We examine the state of diplomacy today, including a number of structural factors affecting multilateral diplomacy. We look briefly at the global phenomena that deserve attention if we are to develop a science of international relations that is fit for purpose. We open a discussion of the structural biases that are a feature of Western modernity in general and US foreign policy in particular.

THE MODERN MULTILATERAL SYSTEM

In September 2018, addressing the UN General Assembly, President Donald Trump commented on 'globalism' and 'global governance' (Trump, 2018, n.p.):

> America is governed by Americans. We reject the ideology of globalism, and we embrace the doctrine of patriotism. Around the world, responsible nations must defend against threats to sovereignty not just from global governance, but also from other, new forms of coercion and domination.

The word 'globalism' is deployed here in such a way as to suggest that efforts to regulate power at the global level are stifling freedom and national identity. Under the slogan 'America First', President Trump is changing the focus of US foreign policy. It is true that many other governments around the world are slow to invest in multilateral cooperation and universal human rights, often from a perspective very different to that of Washington. No other state, however, has played as important a part as the US in shaping the multilateral order that we have now; at the time of writing, no other state is as influential as the US in determining what may happen next.

The current fragility of the multilateral system can be seen through several different lenses – for example, the weak implementation of the Paris Accord on Climate Change, uncertainties surrounding the Iran nuclear deal and the future of arms control, the stalemate in the WTO, the difficulty in achieving a global strategy to contain the spread of the coronavirus, differing priorities in the sphere of human rights, and the absence of international understandings in key areas such as cyber espionage and the regulation of artifical intelligence (AI). Under these difficult circumstances, states are looking inwards to their regions, or to their own national prowess, to protect their interests.

The leader of the G20s Global Solutions Initiative identifies a persistent problem, namely, that the pursuit of selfish interests at the expense of a shared common interest is a challenge at every level of human social organisation (Snower, 2020):'Every attempt to establish cooperation at a larger scale is always vulnerable to being undermined by the selfish behaviour of groups at the smaller scale.'

Under today's conditions, should 'cooperation at a larger scale' include planning for humanity as a whole? Does real meaning attach to relationships and responsibilities at the global level?

To frame an accurate account of what we ought to know and can know in relation to multilevel governance and global trends, we need, first, to adopt a historical perspective. The dangerous trends have been long in the making and have deeper causes than anything that has happened in the current decade.

Today's multilateral system is largely based on President Woodrow Wilson's ambition to 'vindicate the principles of peace and justice in the life of the world', as set out in a major speech in April 1917 preparing the way for US involvement in the Great War (Wilson, 1917b). Earlier in 1917, Wilson had declared the following in the Senate of the US (Wilson, 1917a): 'There must be not a balance of power, but a community of power, not organized rivalries, but an organized Common Peace.'

Wilson used capital letters in 'Common Peace'. His speech mentions elements typical of ancient Greek conceptions of a 'common peace' – the autonomy of peoples, freedom of the seas, an end to entangling alliances, and an awareness of shared benefit. Like the Greeks of the 5th and 4th centuries BCE, Wilson saw the organisation of peace as a political project going far beyond the establishment of procedures for arbitration. Wilson had taught ancient history at Bryn Mawr College. In using the term 'Common Peace' he was placing himself imaginatively in the ancient world, in particular, in the world of Thucydides. Arguably, a 'common peace', for Wilson, is the counterpart at the international level of democratic forms of government.

Under the peace terms proposed by Wilson (1918), the 'common peace' becomes 'a general association of nations ... formed under specific covenants'. Wilson's thinking led to the creation of the League of Nations. Because Congress would not accept the collective security provisions of the Covenant, the US did not join the League. Germany and the Soviet Union were not allowed to join until later. From the beginning, the League lacked the universal membership that would give it broad political authority. It also lacked the means to enforce its decisions. President Wilson's vision underestimated, among other factors, the political significance of economic and trade relationships and the difficulty of implementing the principle of self-determination in a consistent manner.

The failure of the League in the 1930s was one of the factors that led to the outbreak of World War II. Nevertheless, the League of Nations represented a new vision of international order and responded to a growing interest in civil society in the future of international relations. The UN, established in 1945, sought to learn from the weaknesses of the League. Membership was open to all states. A much smaller Security Council was created to take decisions on actions to preserve international peace and security. Within that small group, four 'great powers' and, subsequently, China were given permanent membership and a veto over decisions. Furthermore, Chapter VII of the UN Charter authorised the Security Council to use such armed force as may be necessary (if other measures fail) to 'maintain or restore international peace and security' (Article 42).[1] For this purpose, members of the UN committed to making armed forces, assistance, and facilities available to the Security Council.

The worldwide character of the UN, and its power to take action to enforce its decisions, gave the organisation the authority which the League of Nations lacked – at least in principle. This is not to deny that the major powers sought to preserve their own spheres of influence, or that, in the 21st century, the Security Council's permanent membership, mirroring the immediate post-war distribution of power, has become dangerously unrepresentative of global realities.

Alongside the UN, the Bretton Woods institutions – the IMF and World Bank – were established in 1944 to help rebuild the post-war global economy and to promote international economic cooperation. The General Agreement on Trade and Tariffs (GATT) was established in 1947 to promote international trade; GATT became the WTO in the 1990s. The International Court of Justice (ICJ) was established in 1945 as the judicial organ of the UN.

As its membership grew in the 1960s, mainly as a result of decolonisation, the UN began to focus increasingly on the causes of armed conflict, in particular, under-development, injustice, and the denial of human rights. 'Prevention' and 'peacebuilding' are at the heart of what the UN does in the 21st century.

A whole range of institutions and 'field operations' have come into being under the UN umbrella. To offer just a few examples, in very different fields: the WHO, the Organisation for the Prohibition of Chemical Weapons (OPCW), the United Nations Development Programme (UNDP), the United Nations Educational, Scientific and Cultural Organization (UNESCO), and the Office of the UN High Commissioner for Refugees (UNHCR).

Regional multilateral organisations also began to appear after World War II. The Arab League was established in 1945, and the Council of Europe and NATO in 1949. The OSCE began as a conference in 1973 and went on to become a permanent institution in the 1990s. Outside Europe, besides the Arab League, we have the AU, the Association of South East Asian Nations (ASEAN), the South Asian Association for Regional Cooperation (SAARC), and the Organization of American States (OAS). The UN has established economic (or economic and social) 'commissions' in five regions. The Charter foresees the creation of regional security organisations. In the 21st century, the effectiveness of the UN is likely to depend more and more on the quality of regional and inter-regional cooperation.

One of the most successful multilateral arrangements, and a pillar of the 'liberal international order' established after World War II, is the EU, which is not, strictly speaking, an international organisation. The members of an international organisation remain 'sovereign' in their decisions, though they may defer to a treaty or a tribunal. In the EU, the member states have conferred on institutions of a supranational character the competence to legislate in specified areas. EU citizens are directly represented in one of these institutions, the European Parliament (EP). The European Court of Justice ensures the uniform application of EU law in the member states. This dispensation is innovative; it is often described in terms of 'shared sovereignty'.

THE CHANGING NATURE OF MULTILATERAL DIPLOMACY

A number of structural factors are changing the nature of multilateral diplomacy. Principally, there has been a broadening of the multilateral agenda through the SDGs and the climate change convention, as discussed in Chapter 1. We briefly examine six other factors.

THE IMPACT OF GLOBALISATION

First, the interconnectedness of countries has increased dramatically through the internationalisation of the production and distribution of goods and services.

The form that globalisation has taken since the establishment of the WTO in Marrakech in 1994 has brought many benefits. Adaptive economies (such as Ireland; or on a grand scale, China) have become much more prosperous as a result of global economic integration. According to the World Bank, the percentage of the global population living in what is termed 'absolute poverty' has declined significantly (Rosling, Rosling, and Rosling, 2018).

However, globalisation has also, for very many people, created an 'age of anxiety'. Globalisation is seen by large and growing numbers of people around the world as the principal threat to their future. Such concerns appear well-founded: economic statistics reveal gross disparities in the distribution of benefits and opportunities. The global financial crisis of 2008 demonstrates how quickly financial problems in one region can spread around the world and impact on financial stability, economic development, and trade. The potentially catastrophic consequences of a globalising process unmoored from the claims of justice and effective moral controls are felt in many other sectors, including global public health.

As we write, the coronavirus, and the prospect of further waves of disease in the years to come, are causing fear in every part of the world – fear of poverty, even famine, if economic systems break down, as well as fear of the disease. Reeling from what is often perceived as a weakening of society's moral foundations, the greater part of humanity is left floundering without commonly agreed reference points in a world that grows daily more threatening and unpredictable.

THE GROWING NUMBER OF STATES

The growth in the number of nation states has made the work of multilateral organisations both more complex and more laborious. In 1945, there were fewer than 70 states in the world (of which 51 signed the UN Charter). In 2020, there are 193 members of the UN with two other non-member observer states (the Holy See and the State of Palestine). Enabling each of these to express their views and then seeking consensus among so many different voices has become a daunting task.

THE ROLE OF NON-GOVERNMENTAL ORGANISATIONS (NGOS)

From the 1960s onwards, NGOs have emerged as significant actors in the field of international relations. Organisations such as Greenpeace, Amnesty International, the Campaign for Nuclear Disarmament, and numerous 'Third World' development groups have acquired a greater say in the multilateral debates on issues affecting international peace and security. In the 1990s, NGOs were accorded observer status at the UN. NGOs bring a much-needed, well-informed viewpoint from the 'grass roots'. This enriches the discussion and enlarges the range of potential solutions. However, their straight-talking and unswerving devotion to the truth of their cause often pose uncomfortable dilemmas for state actors.

THE INTERNET AND SOCIAL MEDIA

The Internet has both positive and negative consequences for the conduct of diplomacy. Through online communication, governments can obtain a deeper understanding of the positions and policies of others and do not have to rely solely on what is said at meetings. In principle, this is an advantage.

However, the wider impact of the social media on politics and diplomacy is coming under scrutiny. Previously, responsible media (the 'fourth estate') strove to present a balanced picture, setting out a range of views on any given issue in a generally objective and impartial manner. In the age of social media, this paradigm no longer holds. Many people, particularly young people, now receive their news and information from sources whose views and values mirror their own. Often the social media carry the 'news' without attempting to provide serious, independent journalism. To broaden their appeal (and of course their revenue), they reduce complex debates to simplistic sound bites. The effect of this is to make debates on serious issues confrontational rather than constructive, to entrench differences rather than resolve them, and to close minds rather than open them.

The sheer volume of information on social media also means that some stories do not receive enough attention while others, because of their shock value, receive too much. Meanwhile, special interests, such as well-funded political campaigns, or the agencies of foreign governments, distort the 'market place of ideas' by acting anonymously, using their economic power to ensure blanket coverage of some points of view, or even spreading 'fake news'.

The 2019 documentary film *The Great Hack* examines the activities of Cambridge Analytica. It shows a company combining the harvesting of personal data with manipulative techniques derived from state intelligence agencies. Amplifying the fractures in society for political gain and corporate profit clearly undermines democracy.

The Kenyan writer Nanjala Nyabola explores a range of complex emerging issues in the sphere of 'digital democracy' (Nyabola, 2018). Kenya was under pressure in the 1990s to privatise state-held companies. Safaricom emerged from the break-up of a state monopoly. This private/public corporation, whose major shareholder is Vodafone, has been immensely successful in enabling subscribers to send and receive money on their mobile phones, with beneficial social consequences. However, some government services can now only be accessed through platforms provided by Safaricom (p. 65), and there is evidence that it permits government agencies access to user data (p. 87). A business model of this kind calls for close scrutiny. Similarly, Nyabola draws attention to the reliance of African democracies on the exchange of information through global platforms (Facebook and others) that, by their nature as profit-led companies, do not represent a neutral 'public sphere' as traditionally understood. Another of Nyabola's concerns is that 'Dark Social' (meaning invisible private communication channels) is more and more replacing local language radio as the vehicle for political mobilisation (p. 96).

POPULISM

Modern mass communications have fed the rise of new waves of populism in the first decades of the 21st century. We return below to the question of populism and its causes. To the extent that populism encourages voters to mistrust public institutions, there are inevitable consequences for the conduct of diplomacy.

A PHILOSOPHICAL FACTOR IN THE THREAT TO MULTILATERALISM

Multilateralism is also threatened by a philosophical or ideological factor. In the 1970s and 1980s, two global debates were taking place – the North/South dialogue pursued mainly in Geneva, and the East/West dialogue that took place within the so-called Helsinki process or Conference on Security and Cooperation in Europe (CSCE) – conducted at major meetings in several different capitals. A turning point occurred in the 1990s, when the end of the Cold War and the beginnings of globalisation offered hope of a narrowing of the divide between East and West, and North and South. This sense of accomplishment was best expressed in the following famous claim concerning the emergence of a 'single' world (Fukuyama, 1989, p. 1):

> What we may be witnessing is not just the end of the Cold War, or the passing of a particular period of post-war history, but the end of history as such; that is, the endpoint of man's ideological evolution and the universalization of western liberal democracy as the final form of human government.

The 'end of history' is an ahistorical idea. It is simplistic to understand the 20th century simply in terms of liberal democracy prevailing over fascism and communism. From a military point of view, the defeat of fascism owes more to the Soviet Union than to any other actor. The breakdown of a 'Eurocentric' dynamic in global history is as important in historical terms as the role of the liberal democracies in the two World Wars and in the Cold War.

A priori, the idea of progress towards an 'endpoint' seems to contradict the logic of politics. Any form of government can go badly wrong, absent a culture, an ethic, a set of habits and relationships that in some sense *precede* and *undergird* politics; evil is by definition a shape-shifter. Today, a focus on 'ideological evolution' and its 'endpoint' distracts attention from hunger, environmental degradation, pandemics, weapons proliferation, and other real-world dangers.

A process of trial and error is fruitful; perhaps it is the only way in which human culture and human understanding advance. It should be clear by now, however, that the worldwide promotion of a Western political model will never, of itself, and independently of other choices, guide global society into a problem-solving mode. In the Peace Memorial Museum at Hiroshima, the exhibits demonstrate that the US and the UK made a conscious decision in 1944 not to submit the technologies of mass destruction to international scrutiny or negotiation. A line of continuity runs from this fateful decision, emblematic of an aspiration to global leadership, all the way to 2020. In this perspective, US withdrawal from its climate change commitments and Britain's withdrawal from the European Union (Brexit) have something in common, psychologically speaking. In each case, political campaigns have been organised around iconoclastic messaging in the social media. This messaging discounts the importance of relationships and responsibilities and elevates a self-referential agenda presented in greatly oversimplified fashion as a return to what used to happen in the past.

There is a point to targeting globalism if by 'globalism' we mean a single all-engulfing system in which the particularity of each people's historical experience is denied, and human needs are satisfied only indirectly through the outworking of a narrowly interpreted 'liberal world order'. This is the globalism that gave us the Iraq War of 2003 and the financial crisis, and that leaves us underprepared for so many other challenges. However, to reject globalisation, or 'globalism', if by that we mean to ignore the whole question of how politics are to be conducted at the international level, is not a rational response to our difficulties.

In our concern for human rights, if that is truly our concern, all of us need to *examine the patterns of our behaviour in the light of all that we ought to know and can know*. Among the things that *we ought to know and can know* is that a 'globalising' economy and society requires a global encounter of minds and consciences, and some common decisions – unless we prefer 'the future of life to be decided at random' (Harari, 2018, p. 261).

THE GLOBAL PHENOMENA THAT DESERVE URGENT ATTENTION

Next, we look briefly at the global phenomena that deserve attention if we are to develop a global diplomacy that is fit for purpose.

NATURE

In the present epoch, nature itself – the 'terrestrial' – is relevant to any rational political discourse, according to the French philosopher Bruno Latour (2018). We are dealing with 'an upheaval that is mobilizing the earth system itself'. For Latour, the refusal to act in response to common challenges in the realm of the terrestrial is a flight from reality and responsibility. The end result would be a form of politics that by definition has no ultimate purpose. Pope Francis (*Laudato Si'*, 61 and 161) asserts that 'we have stopped thinking about the goals of human activity'.

Climate change is not the only sphere in which nature is relevant to political and economic discourse. Developments in biophysics and genetics give us the capacity to make changes in the genomes of plants, animals, and human beings. In future, these and other capacities may enable scientists to alter what it means to be human, at least in some respects. It is suspected that conditions in wildlife markets in China contributed to the emergence of the COVID-19 pandemic. A related issue is the trade in animal species, including species protected under the Convention on the International Trade in Endangered Species of Wild Fauna and Flora (CITES).

In the 21st century, more than at any other time in history, human judgement and human choices will determine how future generations will understand 'nature'. On what basis will we make our choices? Neither 'Nature', spelt with a capital 'N', nor our human nature are immune from interference and degeneration.

THE VIRTUAL WORLD

On the Internet, more than 25 billion devices are currently connected, a figure that is predicted to rise into the hundreds of billions. We need strong policies in a whole range of areas: big data ethics, 'editorial' responsibility on-line, cyber espionage, cyber warfare, issues surrounding e-money and virtual currencies, and the social and economic impact of the online world.

Most of the Internet's infrastructure and applications are operated by the private sector across multiple jurisdictions. Preponderant influence is exercised by a handful of US and Chinese companies. This pre-existing domination of the relevant space by a limited number of actors, among whom innovation is constant, is a potential obstacle to the role of public authorities – we might say, to the role of politics itself. A study presented to the UN Secretary General in June 2019 favours the design of a Digital Co-Governance system bringing together public, private, and civic stakeholders (Chehadé and Abusitta, 2019). As currently envisaged, the Digital

Co–Governance system will rely mainly on the voluntary adoption of norms by the relevant actors.

Within the virtual world, AI has implications for human society even more far-reaching than the governance of the Internet. 'Trades' in the stock exchange, investment decisions, and commercial and political messaging are often determined by algorithms. AI research seeks to bring about a 'generally intelligent' AI capable of executing tasks in multiple fields – always on the basis of mathematical interpretations of accumulated data. The impact of these technologies on our economies and societies is greater with each year that passes. Against this background, policy makers around the world are working towards 'principles-based guidance' for the development of AI. For example, the Organisation for Economic Co-operation and Development (OECD), in a document adopted in 2019, identifies five complementary value-based principles for the 'responsible stewardship' of AI, of which the first is that 'AI should benefit people and the planet by driving inclusive growth, sustainable development and well-being' (OECD, 2019). Going beyond principles-based guidance, the General Data Protection Regulation (GDPR) is a regulation in EU law on data protection and privacy applicable since May 2018 (EU, 2016). The GDPR has direct legal force in specific areas of policy. It requires data controllers to design information systems with privacy in mind and specifies the lawful bases on which personal data may be processed.

It will not be easy going forward to establish an appropriate degree of accountability – mechanisms for certification and redress – in the vast, complex, and constantly changing landscape of AI. As Henry Kissinger (2018, n.p.) puts it, '[T]he technological world is preoccupied with commercial vistas of fabulous scale'. Is there even a risk that the explanatory power of AI in defined areas will undermine our understanding of the scope of reason, as described in Chapter 1?

MARKETS AND EQUALITY

If market economics are to remain fit for purpose, an ever-widening range of questions needs answers; for example, the implications for employment of AI, the impact on society of asset purchases by central banks, contested criteria (environmental, social) for investment decisions, the workings of the international financial system, the definition of essential services, the narrow basis of competition law (the short-term consumer interest), the mapping of economically relevant activity (gross domestic product (GDP)), and the question of who is responsible for the social ecosystem on which the market depends (education, law, healthcare, housing, childcare, income support). These questions are made more urgent by the likely impact on the world economy of COVID-19.

Behind all the above questions looms the ever-present shadow of inequality. In the US, Angus Deaton and Anne Case (2020a) have highlighted the part played by inequality in an epidemic of 'deaths of despair' by suicide, alcoholic liver disease, and drug overdose. Even before COVID-19, all-population life expectancy in the US had fallen in recent years for the first time since the influenza pandemic that followed World War I.

Under contemporary conditions, whole populations, or categories within populations, depend on market systems that leave them radically disempowered. In April 2020, the Executive Director of the World Food Programme reported to the UN Security Council that a breakdown of supply systems, made worse by COVID-19, threatens more than 30 countries with widespread famine.

Pope Francis, from the moment of his election, has applied the commandment: 'Thou shalt not kill' to 'an economy of exclusion and inequality' (Pope Francis, 2013, p. 45). In his 2020 Easter Urbi et Orbi message (Francis, 2020), the Pope focusses on the issues of economic sanctions and debt relief:

> In light of the present circumstances, may international sanctions be relaxed, since these make it difficult for countries on which they have been imposed to provide adequate support to their citizens, and may all nations be put in a position to meet the greatest needs of the moment through the reduction, if not the forgiveness, of the debt burdening the balance sheets of the poorest nations.

MIGRATION

In 2017, there were 26 million refugees and asylum seekers throughout the world, and the numbers are increasing. The figure for migrants worldwide is climbing towards 300 million. New factors are in play, for example, environmental degradation in Latin America and political instability in countries like Syria,

Iraq, Afghanistan, Eritrea, and Somalia. The key principles under-lying humanitarian work since World War II have been called into question; security concerns come to the fore, often accompanied by the stereotyping of Muslims. Multi-ethnic societies are under strain. Migration is a contentious electoral issue in the US, Europe, and elsewhere. Governments are finding it difficult to formulate common principles or practical policies commensurate with the challenges. Tensions over migration are likely to continue to grow. The protection of rights is largely based on citizenship, and in many cases, a migrant's route to citizenship is very difficult.

THE WEAPONS INDUSTRY

Can it be assumed that the world's gigantic weapons industry is legitimate? There is a school of thought that weapons in themselves are morally neutral and that wars are caused by people and ideas – by which we generally mean other people and other people's ideas. This argument is increasingly hard to sustain. Military balances and 'equations' are harder and harder to define, with all the dangers that derive from proliferation and uncertainty. The arms industry and the arms trade *in themselves* distort public policy and represent a huge opportunity cost.

DEMOCRACY

Facing into the future with philosophical maps that are not up to date, the citizens of many democracies are finding it harder to 'see' the society to which they belong, to agree on the factual basis of public policy, and to form an estimate of the international condi-tions that partly determine every country's domestic options.

Many issues, such as climate change, international trade, and inter-national finance, are governed by multilateral treaties and arrange-ments over which most states have little influence individually. If citizens lose out, they look to their governments for redress. But very often there is little those governments can do by themselves. This breeds disaffection and creates fertile ground for the growth of populism and intolerance.

Populism drives people to the extremities of the political spec-trum because they doubt their capacity to defend successfully a more moderate position. In some countries, the roles of democratic pillars, such as parliament and the judiciary, are being called into question by populists who insist that 'the will of the people' as expressed in a general election is all, and should be respected regardless of constitutional proprieties. With the rise of 'populism', there is a drift in the direction of 'symbolic politics' – a strong attachment to images, formulations, or 'memes' that elicit powerful emotions and serve as a psychological refuge, while adding little or nothing to democratic deliberation.

In some areas, such as international trade and finance, arms control, and perhaps now the control of disease, we seem unable to work together effectively on a global level. In principle, regional approaches are part of the necessary response. But the wrong kind of 'regionalism' can lead to new rivalries.

THE STRUCTURAL BIASES OF WESTERN MODERNITY

In this book we envisage a multilayered global conversation aimed at reappropriating basic political values and strengthening community at different levels of political organisation. An *examined* political life, open to all facts and all sources of wisdom, is the point at which to begin.

We will conclude this chapter with a reflection on how our *obligation to know* raises a fundamental question concerning *the vantage point* from which we study society. 'Turning away quite leisurely from the disaster' and 'large-scale structural biases', as discussed at the beginning of this chapter, are not just a casual feature of our cultures and civilisations.

At the very beginning of the Western tradition, Homer's gods take a close interest in certain aspects of human conduct. It is worthy of divine attention that Agamemnon and Achilles quarrel, threatening the social code of a warrior aristocracy. The captives and slave-concubines passed around as prizes among the Greek leaders are of much less interest to the gods.

The 'limited coverage' offered by ancient systems of ethics is exacerbated by another factor. In the moral systems of Greece and Rome, actions tended to be judged, not by their character or essence as actions, but by the image and status of the actor in the eyes of his peers – his role, his motives, his inner equilibrium. Here, from the account of Julius Caesar's campaigns in Gaul, is a passage in which an act of primitive savagery is explained away because it supposedly does not define Caesar's character:

> His clemency was so well known that no one would think him a cruel man if for once he took severe measures. So, he decided to deter all others by making an example of the defenders of Uxellodunum. All who had borne arms had their hands cut off and were then let go.
>
> (*De Bello Gallico*, VIII 43)

In ancient societies, the 'rules of reciprocity', in Montesquieu's terms, are developed through a sifting process in which hierarchies and exclusions are gradually defined and property rights are consolidated. 'Justice' comes to mean primarily the regulation of partnership (Aristotle, *Politics* I.1). Other relationships, including external relationships, do not qualify as aspects of partnership and are therefore not covered by the prevailing understanding of 'justice'. The logic of this narrow vision of society is that the long-term survival of a successful political arrangement becomes, for its beneficiaries, the ultimate measure of value. This opens up a broad path to self-deception:

> Using false names, they refer to robbery, murder, and slave-dealing (*auferre trucidare rapere*) as 'an imperial system'; when they make a desert, they call it 'peace'.
>
> (Tacitus, 1967, 30.4)

In the past, European societies and the US saw themselves, to a significant degree, as ancient Roman lookalikes, asserting the 'destiny' of their own nations. Thomas Jefferson framed Roman-style institutions (the Senate, the Capitol) to enable the 'pursuit of happiness'. In parallel, Jefferson strongly upheld the institution of slavery and overlooked the impact of his Roman ideals on the indigenous peoples of America. The great classicist and Nobel Prize winner Theodor Mommsen, an important influence on late 19th-century German politics, idolised Julius Caesar: 'Caesar was the entire and perfect man … the historian, when once in a thousand years he falls in with the perfect, can only be silent regarding it' (Mommsen and Dickson, 2019, Book V, Chapter XI). Mommsen adds that 'Cromwell is of all statesmen perhaps the most akin to Caesar'. In 1919, following the Great War, the service personnel of 12 allied countries received a Victory Medal showing a winged, full-length classical figure.

The next of kin of every British soldier killed in the war received a medallion featuring another classically inspired image, a helmeted Britannia holding a trident.

The 'Roman' or 'classical' self-image of Western societies as agents of a 'higher civilisation' is an important underlying factor in the cultural concept of 'modernity'. 'Modernity' traditionally refers to modes of social organisation which emerged in Europe from about the 17th century and became worldwide in their influence (Giddens, 1990). Under the influence of Roman ideas, we have been tempted in the 'West' to see our own world as the highest rung on a ladder of development.

In reality, the ventures of powerful Western societies have included forms of exploitation and interference with others' rights that are in conflict with any coherent account of progress and enlightenment. The concept of a 'law of nations' (*ius gentium*) was revived in the 16th century largely as an attempt to restrain Spain's exploitation of indigenous peoples. William Dalrymple's *The Anarchy: The Relentless Rise of the East India Company*, published in 2019, demonstrates that the East India Company, that seminal colonial venture, corrupted politics at Westminster through bribery, extracted wealth from India using brutal methods, and was a rent-seeking association, if 'rent' means a scale of rewards that bears no relationship to the work done or any conceivable common good.

In what precedes, we have looked briefly at the 'Western' or European tradition. 'Structural biases' are present in other cultures as well; under a false 'algebra of justice' (Arundhati Roy), the forms of human suffering are weighed or discarded in line with the self-interest of a dominant group. Our counterstrategy is to bring to mind the victims of history and to delve more deeply into our religious and philosophical heritage in search of a clearer understanding of political processes: 'only he who knows the empire of might and knows how not to respect it is capable of love and justice' (Weil, 1952, p. 53).

This brings us back to the question of our vantage point. The perspective that we choose is inseparable from our self-understanding, our priorities, our receptivity to other points of view, even our moral character. One of the most important ways in which religion can contribute to global diplomacy is by *altering the focus of our attention*. In the Quran, according to a recent study, 'the social nature of the human being is part of the wisdom of God's creation' (in Nasr, 2002, p. 159):

> There is no secret conference of three but He is their fourth, nor of five but He is their sixth, nor of less than that or more but He is with them wherever they may be (58:7).

A social scientist would describe shared 'social meaning' in a different way. She would tell us, perhaps, that the adaptations in lifestyle through which we may be able to respond effectively to climate change or a global pandemic require the habitual assent of a great number of individuals.

A question for religious believers and social scientists alike is this: who or what defines the community that gives rise to a shared social meaning? We return in Chapter 4 to this touchstone of public truth.

NOTE

1 United Nations, *Charter of the United Nations*, www.un.org>charter> united-nations.

REFERENCES

Amer, K., and Noujaim, J. (Directors). (2019). *The Great Hack* [Documentary movie]. United States. Netflix.

Aristotle. (1932). *Politics*, translated by H. Rackham. Loeb Classical Library. Cambridge: Harvard University Press.

Auden, W.H. (1976). 'Musée des Beaux Arts,' in E. Mendelson (ed.), *W.H Auden: Collected Poems*. London: Faber and Faber.

Caesar, J. (1917). *The Gallic War*, translated by H.J. Edwards. Loeb Classical Library. Cambridge: Harvard University Press.

Chehadé, F., and Abusitta, N. (2019). 'Digital Norms: Co-Governance for a Trusted Digital World.'Viewed from https://blogs.bsg.ox.ac.uk/wp-content/uploads/2019/02/DIGITAL-NORMS-Chehade-Abusitta-JAN19-1.pdf

Dalrymple, W. (2019). *The Anarchy: The Relentless Rise of the East India Company*. London: Bloomsbury

Deaton, A. and Case, A. (2020). *Deaths of Despair and the Future of Capitalism*. Princeton: Princeton University Press.

EU. 2016.Viewed from https://gdpr-info.eu

Francis. (2013). *Evangelii Gaudium*.Vatican:Vatican Press.

Francis. (2015). *Laudato Si'*.Vatican:Vatican Press.

Francis. (2020). 'Easter "Urbi et Orbi" Message and Blessing.' Viewed from www.vatican.va>content>messages>urbi

Fukuyama, F. (1989). 'The End of History?' *The National Interest*, 16, 3–18.

Giddens, A. (1990). *The Consequences of Modernity*. Stanford: Stanford University Press.

Griffin, M. (1976). *Seneca: A Philosopher in Politics*. Oxford: Oxford University Press.

Harari, Y.N. (2018). *21 Lessons for the 21st Century*. London: Jonathan Cape.

Kissinger, H. (2018). 'How the Enlightenment Ends,' *Atlantic*, June 2018.

Latour, B. (2018). *Down to Earth: Politics in the New Climatic Regime*. Cambridge: Polity Press (French edition, 2017).

Mommsen, T. and Dickson, W.P. (translator). (2019). *The History of Rome*. Good Press: Kindle Edition (first published in German, 1854–1856).

Nasr, S.H. (2002). *The Heart of Islam: Enduring Values for Humanity*. New York. HarperCollins.

Nyabola, N. (2018). *Digital Democracy, Analogue Politics: How the Internet Era Is Transforming Kenya (African Arguments)*. London: Zed Books.

OECD. (2019). OECD Principles on AI. Viewed from www.oecd.org/going-digital/ai/principles/

Rosling, H., Rosling, A., and Rosling, A. (2018). *Factfulness: Ten Reasons We're Wrong about the Word: And Why Things Are Better Than You Think*. London: Sceptre.

Roy, A. (2001). *The Algebra of Infinite Justice*. New Delhi: Penguin Books India (Viking).

Snower, D. J. (2020) *Awakening in the Post-Pandemic World*. Blog, Washington, DC: Brookings.

Tacitus. (1967). *De Vita Agricolae*, edited by R.M. Ogilvie and I. Richmond. Oxford: Clarendon Press.

Thucydides. (1996). *The Landmark Thucydides: A Comprehensive Guide to the Peloponnesian War* (revised edition of the Richard Crawley translation), edited by R.B. Strassler. New York: Free Press.

Trump, D. (2018). 'Remarks by President Trump to the 73rd Session of the UN General Assembly.' September 25, New York. Viewed from www.whitehouse.org

Weil, S. (1952). *Intimations of Christianity among the Ancient Greeks*. London: Routledge & Kegan Paul.

Wilson, W. (1917a). 'Address to the Senate.' January 22, Washington, DC.

Wilson, W. (1917b). 'War Message to Congress.' April 2, Washington, DC.

Wilson, W. (1918). 'Message to Congress.' January 8, Washington, DC.

TOWARDS THE GLOBAL
OBJECTIVE OF A COMMON
PEACE FOR HUMANITY

IMAGING OR VISUALISING PEACE

Our second axiom, which is the focus of this chapter, is that we need to '*image*' *or visualise peace as the rightful possession of the human community as a whole*. St Augustine speaks for all civilisations when he argues that 'there is no man who does not wish for peace' (*City of God*, XIX.12). 'Even when men wish a present state of peace to be disturbed', he continues, 'they do so not because they hate peace, but because they desire the present peace to be exchanged for one that suits their wishes.'

By its nature, the desire for peace becomes a desire for universal peace. Half a century ago, in 1974, Alexander Solzhenitsyn explored this dynamic in his Nobel speech:[1]

> World literature has it in its power to convey condensed experience from one land to another so that we might cease to be divided and blinded, so that the different scales of values might be made to agree, and so that one nation might learn correctly and concisely the true history of another with as much strength of recognition and painful awareness as if it had itself experienced that history; in this way, it might be spared from repeating the same cruel mistakes. And perhaps under

such conditions we artists will be able to cultivate within ourselves a field of vision to embrace the WHOLE WORLD: observing like any other human being that which lies nearby, and beginning to draw in what is happening in the rest of the world. And we shall correlate, and we shall have a global perspective.

The great cultural traditions of humanity, each in its own way, participate in Solzhenitsyn's hope. When we observe what is nearby, we 'begin to draw in' what is happening in the rest of the world.

Solzhenitsyn's insight is as old as the Bible:

I have given him [my servant] my spirit so that he can open up true discernment to all peoples ... Look, I have chosen you ... to be the light of nations, for a salvation that reaches to the ends of the earth.

(Isaiah 42:1–2 and 49:6)

Alexander the Great's campaign of conquest led to the emergence of new forms of connectivity across a vast region of the world. Greek philosophical schools began to question the status of the citizen-state as the primary expression of human community (Lane, 2014). The Stoic philosopher Zeno developed the ideal of the *kosmopolitēs* or global citizen. Among the Stoics, local forms of citizenship were still taken seriously. However, as citizens of the *kosmos*, we have an additional perspective which must always be taken into account when we make political decisions.

Religious and philosophical traditions come together when Philo of Alexandria (1902) draws on Zeno for his portrait of Moses:

He is a kosmopolitēs, for which reason he is not listed on the citizen-list of any city ... he has received no parcel of land but the whole world as his portion.

(*Vita Mosis*: Life of Moses, 1.157)[2]

Today, 'the universal dimension of our civic responsibility' (Camdessus, 2019a) is demonstrable in fact. Climate risks, pandemics, the need for stable currencies, migration, development finance, the role of AI, the threat posed by new forms of violence, and many other challenges require global strategies.

In this chapter, we will explore the traditions of ancient Greece, Israel, China, and India for glimpses of how religious and philosophical thinkers visualised, or imaged, a state of general peace as the proper goal of politics. Multilateral diplomacy, as described in

Chapter 2, has its roots in ancient ideals. We aim to demonstrate that the concept of a 'common peace', if we examine it closely, has particular attributes that deserve our close attention.

THE AXIAL AGE

In the so-called Axial Age, beginning around the 8th century BC, humanity was learning for the first time to verify by experience and articulate its political values. In many different civilisations, there emerged a social, political, and juridical space in which old ways of doing things could be examined critically and new conventions could be established. Very often, the 'felt absence' (German: *Abwesenheit*[3]) of justice was the factor that led to the critique of existing orthodoxies. The principle of verification produced a step change in terms of political transparency and accountability. In addition, it contributed to forms of experimental science, new technologies such as ship building, the opening of markets, and the use of coinage. Kindred developments in different spheres, taken together, represented a civilisational shift or transition.

In Confucian thought, the term 'grand union' describes an imagined society, in which 'a public and common spirit ruled all under the sky'. According to Confucius and his successors, we should work to ensure that our existing society, the 'small tranquillity', approximates, progressively, to the imagined ideal. In this perspective, leadership is a form of service to the community (Chan, 2014, p. 10).

In the prophetic and wisdom traditions of Israel, God does not create chaos or intend life in society to be unliveable. Public service is an important value. In the time of Solomon, responsibility is exercised top-down by educated court officials. In later periods, the critique of power from below acquires great importance. The anger of the prophet Amos at the workings of impersonal economic forces can be felt across the centuries:

> Listen to this, you who trample on the poor and gain power over the helpless ... who say, 'we can overcharge, use false measures' ... or 'we will get a slave through having in our power a poor man who can't find even the price of a pair of sandals to pay us off'.

> (Amos 8:4–6)

In India, the Buddha breaks with an inherited conglomerate of political, economic, and religious power, crystallising a tradition of dissent (the Sramana or Samana tradition) that has deep origins in Indian society (Gandhi, 1999, p. 39). In the 3rd century BC, in a development of the Buddhist tradition, the Emperor Ashoka promotes peace through dharma, the inner law that shapes all being, and is, at the same time, a humane code of conduct embracing all aspects of life (Thapar, 1961). Ashoka commissions a series of inscriptions, the so-called Rock Edicts and Pillar Edicts, to make known the elements of dharma throughout his domains. One of the most famous of these inscriptions, the 4th Rock Edict, proclaims that 'the sound of the drum has become the sound of dharma'. Formerly, drums were used for leading forces into battle; now, according to the king, the population will be organised for peaceful purposes.

In 5th-century Athens, Socrates and other thinkers responded to the breakdown of human communities by asking a series of structural questions about politics and human nature. The Greeks perceived an analogy between politics and the emerging science of medicine: the better we understand how political and social systems work, the more we can become agents of change. 'Therapy of the common interest' (*therapeuein ta koina*) is a political term of art (Thucydides, 1996, III.82:8). Lawgiving and justice are described by Socrates (Plato, *Gorgias*, 464 B–C) as 'political therapy' (*therapeia tēs politikēs*).

The examples that we have used from the Axial Age – Confucianism, the prophetic traditions of Israel, Buddhism, and Greek political science – suggest that suffering and division do not have the decisive word in human history. Civilisational values can change for the better over time. That change can be sustained through centuries.

In the Axial Age, a religion or worldview is interwoven in the process of change. Often, a religious tradition emerges from an epoch of change with a clearer self-understanding. Is the 'state of nature' a war of all against all? Or are we disposed 'by nature' to a creative, cooperative way of life in harmony with the 'natural world'? The pathfinding thinkers of the first millennium BCE offer hopeful answers to such questions.

Many aspects of the Axial Age are open to debate. The degree to which developments at different times and places are interconnected

is disputed, as is the degree to which other societies, less well studied, have developed similar ideas to ancient Greece, or India, or
China. In any case, civilisations can no longer be seen as walled off
from one another and self-sufficient:

> Knowledge systems that have governed world history have no single
> source. Thus, the direction taken by mathematics, astronomy, and med-
> icine evolved from an intersection of ideas that were Chinese, Indian,
> Greek, and Arab, and these were developed further in Europe.
>
> (Thapar, 2008)

For some of the leading exponents of the Axial Age, it was important
to visualise the various earlier civilisations as tributaries flowing into
an 'achieved' Western civilisation, as they saw it at the time. The question of 'impact' arises in a different way when we compare the Axial
Age to other major patterns in history. The conquests of Alexander
the Great began a process of globalisation in the Mediterranean, the
Middle East, and Asia as far as the Oxus. The Roman Empire, bor-
rowing from Alexander, developed a formidable political narrative
of its own. For the purposes of this book, it is not necessary to settle
the arguments around parallels, connections, continuity, and relative
impact. The Axial Age is the template, not the taproot, for the *prise
de conscience* at the global level for which we advocate in this book.

What happened in the Axial Age, viewed as a template, can be
compared to what has begun to happen in modern Western society
since women acquired the right to vote. Ultimately, the change is not
a matter of one or two specific reforms – that women vote or achieve
top positions within powerful institutions. Nor does the emancipation of women, in itself, enable the development of new forms of
governance at the global level. What the emancipation of women
implies in the longer run is a changing disposition – an end to patri-
archy, new role models for young people, more enlightened social
priorities, and a better understanding of what power really is. This can
fairly be described as a process having anthropological significance.

EIGHT KEY CONCEPTIONS REGARDING
THE NATURE OF PEACE

The great civilisations of the Axial Age share a number of key
conceptions regarding the nature of peace. By way of provoking a

discussion, we will develop eight mutually supportive ideas, inspired by both ancient and modern experience.

PEACE IS THE NORM

First comes the hope that destructive division will not have the last word in human history. Peace is the norm. A state of general or common peace is the proper goal of politics. In their search for a conception of equilibrium in society, Greek writers use analogies based on musical composition, the harmony between organs of the body, and mathematical equations. Today, the Institute for Economics and Peace (IEP) in Sydney has developed a metric for assessing the attitudes, institutions, and structures that sustain peaceful societies. This is sometimes referred to as a systems approach: a well-functioning government, the rule of law, low levels of corruption, and a strong business environment interact with factors such as access to information, respect for others, and the effective distribution of wealth to make for a flourishing system or 'ecology'. To achieve 'positive peace', we need to look for improvements in relation to all the main indicators or pillars on which peace depends.

FREEDOM IS CORRELATIVE WITH LEGITIMATE AUTHORITY OR LEADERSHIP

In addressing point two, a good place from which to start is that, in Confucian thought, channels of communication and consultation enable political leaders to demonstrate that they are at the service of the people, and the people themselves to develop trust in their political leaders: the 'perfecting' of relationships is centrally important (Chan, 2014).

In the *Prometheus Bound* of Aeschylus, Zeus, who dominates, and Prometheus, in chains, are essentially equal – both are Titans. What is missing in their interaction is freedom: Prometheus has been nailed to a rock by agents of Zeus whose names are Power and Force. At stake in the drama is whether a relationship based on freedom – mutual willing consent (*hekōn hekonti*) – can be restored at some point in the deep future.

In Thucydides, war is a 'savage teacher' (*biaios didaskalos*), lowering people's horizons to the problem of mere survival (Thucydides, 1996, III.82:2). At its best, on the other hand, political life is an education (*paideia*) that introduces us to life in community. The theme of the Funeral Oration of Pericles, history's most influential statement of the democratic ideal, is that to engage with others in creating a common life can become an expression of love. There is a read-across to 'Confucian perfectionism'.

The connotations of Hebrew terms such as *shalom* ('peace and human flourishing'), *hèsed*, (loving kindness and equity'), and *tsedakah* ('justice-with-mercy') point towards a vision of peace as bringing out the personal maturity that we discussed in Chapter 1.

In St Augustine, we turn to social organisation because we are similar to one another in what we love (like Zeno's 'cosmopolitans'):

> If one should say, 'A people is the association of a multitude of rational beings united by a common agreement on the objects of their love,' then it follows that to observe the character of a particular people we must examine the objects of its love.
>
> (*City of God*, XIX.24)

In the Axial Age, freedom often came to be understood as the condition of authentic human relationships based on good will. Freedom and force are discordant; freedom and legitimate leadership are correlative.

TRUTH IN ALL ITS FORMS IS THE CONCERN OF POLITICS

To reflect on our third point, before his death the Buddha addresses his disciples as follows:

> 'You must be your own lamps, your own refuges ... Hold firm to the truth as a lamp and a refuge' (conversation with Ananda in the Digha Nikaya, quoted by Gandhi, 1999, p. 37).

Siddhartha Gautama – the Buddha – engages with individuals at all levels of society to enable them to see that the brutal power politics of the Magadha kingdom and the ramifications of the caste system do not express any ultimate truth about human nature.

For the prophet Zechariah, the ability to 'see' to form a right judgement about a shared situation is the gift of a 'spirit of kindness and mercy ... a pure Spirit' (12:10, 13:2). Below are some lines from the second chapter of Zephaniah (verse 3):

> Seek the Lord,
> all you, the humble of the earth ...

Practise discernment
seek justice.

In the Second Letter to the Thessalonians (2:7), St Paul speaks of the mystery of iniquity at work in the world. Iniquity (in Latin, *iniquitas*; in Greek, *anomia*) suggests not so much the absence of law as the presence of a distorted law – a law confused and corrupted by a dangerous admixture of untruth. One is reminded of Shelley's (2003, p. 401) 'Mask of Anarchy':

Last came Anarchy: he rode
On a white horse, splashed with blood;
He was pale even to the lips,
Like Death in the Apocalypse.
And he wore a kingly crown;
And in his grasp a sceptre shone;
On his brow, this mark I saw –
'I AM GOD, AND KING, AND LAW!

In many biblical texts, the just man (Greek: *dikaios*) is the standard, in fact the only standard, by which iniquity, or false law, or not-law can be revealed for what it is. In both the Septuagint and the New Testament, the just person's capacity for true judgement is rendered by the word *krima* or *krisis* (including in Isaiah and Zephaniah, as quoted above).

Even in ancient societies firmly based on top-down rule, such as the Persian Empire, the freedom to speak the truth or even to act independently in the light of the truth represents the cultural ideal. In Xenophon's 4th century BCE biography of Persia's King Cyrus, the king has two good counsellors – Hystaspes and Chrysantas (*Cyropaedia*, Book IV). The first obeys the king willingly. The second, even more to be admired, carries out, without instructions, 'what he himself sees it was better for us to have done'. Friendship and truth are linked values within this idealised picture of the administration of Cyrus.

THE NEED TO NURTURE OUR PRE-POLITICAL CULTURE

Fourth, our capacity for loyal opposition, our ability to stand back and criticise in the common interest, depends on the quality of our 'pre-political culture' – of a social reality antecedent to political engagement. Out of a private space come political and social engagement – the ability to intervene with others to change the social dynamic and build communities.

Aeschylus and other figures of the Athenian Golden Age speak of the innate 'reverence' (*deos, aidōs*) on which the practice of politics depends. For Pericles in the Funeral Oration, there is already an important 'private' side to the Athenian project: the democratic constitution underpins a whole way of life, much of which takes place in the home, at festivals, and in the theatre, away from politics.

In the Hebrew tradition, the covenant is antecedent to any political arrangement. In India, the *shramana dharma* (way of life) involves distancing oneself from the political and economic powers-that-be in order to have the freedom to promote social justice. In this respect, there is a line of continuity from Buddhism, through the Bhakti sants, the Sufis within Islam, and the Sikhs, all the way to Mahatma Gandhi.

THE IMPORTANCE OF DIALOGUE

Fifth, to build a 'common peace' where it does not yet exist, we need to understand the nature of dialogue. The aim of ancient Greek or Indian philosophical dialogue was to bring intellectual coherence to a potentially chaotic environment by defining the principal arguments in play and bringing these arguments into contact with one another. Greek writers pictured the common logos or 'shared account of how things are' (Heraclitus, 1957, Fragments 1, 2, and 50). To understand what is at stake, let us look at a recent statement from an American scholar of international relations (Mandelbaum, 2019, p. 144):

> If Russia, China, and Iran were to adopt, by whatever route, fully democratic political systems including both popular sovereignty and the protection of economic, religious, and political liberty, the need for nationalist assertion as a source of legitimacy would shrivel.

Like many other American scholars, Mandelbaum operates with a presumption that democracies, almost by definition, are less aggressive than other states. Thucydides would smile: a lifetime comparing Athens to Sparta did not lead him to this conclusion.

Mandelbaum sees the post-Cold War period (between 1990 and 2015) as an era of peace largely attributable to the 'benign hegemony of the United States' (Mandelbaum, 2019, p. 136). The principal obstacle to a future world free of 'security competition' is constituted by three countries – Russia, China, and Iran – whose governments, according to Mandelbaum, are acting out of false motives. The US is in a different category because of the 'liberties' that it promotes (no distinction is made between the categories of religious, political, and economic freedom).

Mandelbaum is moderate in comparison with some American thinkers; he does not countenance undermining or overthrowing the governments that stand in the way of his ideas. Nevertheless, he embodies some of that 'existential mistrust' to which we referred in Chapter 1, in that he does not appear to accept Moscow, Beijing, or Tehran (or, by implication, many others) as valid dialogue partners.

In his speech when he received the Charlemagne Prize in 2016, Pope Francis said the following:

> There is an impression that Europe is tending to become increasingly 'entrenched', rather than open to initiating new social processes capable of engaging all individuals and groups in the search for new and productive solutions to current problems.

Governments should acknowledge that every time they say of a critic or an opponent, 'if he is not a hundred percent right, he may be ten or twenty percent right', they are creating a space in which trust can develop, and international society can begin to find 'new and productive solutions to current problems'.

THE VALUE OF FRIENDSHIP

Sixth, political society is promoted to a great extent by friendship, by what we choose to do for its own sake. Aristotle examines the role of friendship in politics in great depth and detail in Books VIII and IX of the *Nicomachean Ethics*. Using the example of travelling companions, he argues that our pursuit of a common project tends as a matter of experience to turn into friendship (*philia*). The 'shared journey' of the travelling companions becomes a metaphor for community in all its forms: the family, soldiers on campaign together, men embarked on a business venture, religious festivals at the local level, and finally, the *polis* or citizen-state itself.

In the political community, the detailed provisions of the law become less important as friendship takes root (*Nicomachean Ethics*,

VIII.1). Friendship even leads to self-sacrificing actions that contradict self-interest as ordinarily understood. In 2020, Aristotle's discussion of the role of friendship in political life is a lens through which to study the levels of 'social capital' available in different societies as we struggle with COVID-19.

THE TEST OF CIVILISATION IS THE ABILITY TO INTEGRATE NEW PEOPLE AND IDEAS

In terms of the seventh point, Homer is famously impartial between the Greeks and Trojans. Aeschylus writes a play, with Pericles as producer, in which the very recent Persian invasion is looked at through Persian eyes. Thucydides notes that foreigners are in attendance as Pericles delivers the Funeral Oration. Sparta's expulsion of foreigners is one of the issues at stake at the outbreak of the Peloponnesian War (Thucydides, 1996, I.144.2).

Indian civilisation is a confluence of many streams – tribal or indigenous cultures; religious writings in Sanskrit and Tamil; Buddhism and the other religious traditions growing out of Hinduism; the multifaceted culture of the Mughals; the Persian influence on the languages of North India; Gandhi and the struggle for independence; the great works of creative literature in several languages, including English; European influences that include British law; and economic globalisation.

When Virgil is asked to write an epic poem to celebrate the greatness of Rome, he builds the story around a refugee driven by fate, whose task is to journey from Troy into the unknown, accompanied by a remnant of his people and preserving only his religion, the essence of the old way of life; everything else changes. Aeneas's journey ends in Latium in Italy. There he founds a new realm based on the coexistence of Trojans, Latins, Greeks, and Etruscans.

The post-war European project draws on deep cultural sources in the attempt to re-create a European civilisation based on forgiveness of the past and allegiance freely given to a future common good. The revived Europe, according to its own ideals, shares with the humanism of the early Renaissance the ability to offer hospitality to many different strands of history and culture, including, since the fall of the Berlin Wall, a large number of new member states.

According to its own ideals, Europe is 'dynamic', aiming at an economy of solidarity at home and abroad. The most important early statement of the European ideal is the Schuman Declaration of May 1950,[4] which contains the following sentence:

> With increased resources, Europe will be able to pursue the achievement of one of its essential tasks, namely, the development of the African continent.

As so often happens, one day's moral imperative is the future's compelling political logic. The population of Africa may exceed the population of Europe several times over by the end of the present century. To turn the encounter of cultures and peoples across the Mediterranean into a journey that enriches us all will be a central challenge of the decades ahead.

ENLARGING THE COMMON SPACE

Eighth, and finally, the desire for peace, unless, in St Augustine's famous phrase, it is a *magnum latrocinium* (a 'vast conspiracy among thieves'), broadens into the desire for a common peace.

Ashoka's 13th Rock Edict expresses the idea of 'conquest by dharma', instead of by war or violence (Thapar, 1961, pp. 256–257). The adoption of the principles of dharma by neighbouring states creates a common moral space.

Zeno and the Stoics, as mentioned above, taught that for the wise there exists in principle a global order, a *kosmos*. One of Plutarch's moral essays describes Alexander the Great as a philosopher in action whose policy was to reconcile peoples and civilisations. In this connection, Plutarch summarises the Stoic vision of a global society (*Moralia*, 329 a–c):

> all the inhabitants of this world should not live differentiated by their respective rules of justice into separate cities and communities ... we should consider all men to be of one community and one polity, and we should have a common life and an order common to us all, even as a herd that feeds together and shares the pasturage of a common field.

A national political community is an energy system that inevitably comes into contact with other energy systems: unless this contact is mediated by customs, agreements, and formats for dialogue, it is easy to predispose ourselves to aggression through an inward-looking, truth-distorting, historical narrative marked by 'existential mistrust'.

INDEPENDENT SHARED VALUES

Our *eight characteristics of peace*, discussed above, can be understood as facets of an evolving process, namely, creating and sustaining independent, shared values, and a vocabulary to support them, through acts of solidarity and frameworks for dialogue, as well as legally binding decisions. Such values are shared, because moral norms are above any individual; and they are independent, because moral norms are more than social conventions. Our *'characteristics of peace'* demonstrate that the 'granular' provisions of established law are an inadequate foundation for society, for several inescapable reasons.

The law is incomplete. To take what we can within the limits of the law is not necessarily right. For ancient writers, limits on the pursuit of gain are defined by 'unwritten law'.

The lawgiver will not have reckoned with the precise circumstances of every case. Any law should therefore be applied in a 'personal' way, with discernment and an element of mercy.

Background circumstances change. In times of political upheaval, a citizen's obligations under the law can become unclear. Do we serve a revolutionary government? How do we define our obligations under rapidly changing international circumstances?

That citizens have regard for one another, or that nations trust one another, is an outcome of politics, not a 'constitutive choice' within the political process. 'Fraternity' is elusive – harder to achieve than 'liberty' or 'equality'. In the light of the constant interaction between independent, shared values and the granular provisions of the law, we can state that political values fall into three baskets:

1. 'Pre-political values' are the ideas and approaches – the orientation, the methodology, the world view, and the axioms of the historical imagination – with which we approach politics.
2. By political values, we mean laws, treaties, and concrete policies. Political values are often 'granular'.
3. In the realm of 'post-political values', we can place, for example, the strengthening of friendship and solidarity that can arise as a result of the right political decisions.

The instinct of ancient civilisations is that society is held together, ultimately, by a sense of the sacred; hence, the emphasis placed by ancient cultures on dharma, custom, decorum, rites and rituals, the sacredness of oaths, and the inviolability of sanctuaries. Serious politics means giving due weight to the realm of religion and human values.

'IF YOU WANT PEACE, WORK FOR JUSTICE'

In his message for the World Day of Peace in 1972, Pope Paul VI called for 'a new expression of Justice, a new foundation for Peace'. The central idea is that persons in 'posts of responsibility' should avoid the temptation to impose rules by force. In any given group – a family, a school, a workplace, a community, a city, a state – 'normal relations' should be established in a manner that respects the dignity and free-dom of each person. Drawing on the saying of the prophet Isaiah that the fruit of justice is peace (32:17), Pope Paul formulated the maxim, 'If you want peace, work for justice'. In this choice of words, there is an implied allusion to a very different Roman maxim cited by a military writer of the 4th century CE: 'if you want peace, prepare for war'.[5]

Working for justice, achieving the global objective of a common peace for humanity, removing mere force from our political equa-tions, and delivering democracy are ultimately one and the same struggle, if we accept the following definition of democracy, offered by Pope Benedict XVI (2006):[6]

> Democracy will be fully implemented only when all individuals and all peoples have access to life, food, water, healthcare, education, work, and certainty of their rights, through an ordering of internal and external relations that guarantees everyone a chance to participate.

A MEDIUM-TERM PERSPECTIVE

On what time scale should we pursue an 'age of sharing', an Axial Age at the planetary level?

The Israeli historian Yuval Noah Harari has written three best-selling books on the past and future of our species. Harari's narrative begins with the appearance of matter and energy 13.5 billion years ago and passes via the origins of organic life 3.8 billion years ago to the start of human history perhaps about 70,000 years ago with the development of language. In this long perspective, Harari sees the present century as a turning point. Through biological engineering and other interventions, we may soon be able to bring about physiological changes and changes in consciousness that will call human identity into question. For Harari, this breaking free of biologically determined limits is even more significant than the destruction of the environment and the proliferation of nuclear weapons. Below is a summation of one of Harari's (2014, pp. 415–416) key conclusions:

> We are more powerful than ever before, but have very little idea what to do with all that power ... Self-made gods with only the laws of physics to keep us company, we are accountable to no one ... Is there anything more dangerous than dissatisfied and irresponsible gods who don't know what they want?

The premise of this book is that we have reached a 'point of inflection' in international affairs and that the moral and political vacuum pinpointed by Harari represents a clear and present danger. The challenge is to prevent impersonal forces from shaping events and compromising our planetary future.

That said, do we expect in the 21st century, or in any foreseeable future, to bring about a lasting, all-encompassing political system of the kind dreamt of in ancient Rome? Or should we focus, not on a new Pax Romana, but in the medium-term – on what can be achieved within the next generation – by seeking to harmonise religious, cultural, political, and economic factors as best we can in order to extend, where needed, a shared form of historical literacy and a capacity for common action?

Many religious voices have encouraged the idea that the United Nations is a providential initiative, a 'necessary path' presenting itself just as humanity has come to a historical crossroads. Addressing the UN General Assembly during the hope-filled post-war era, Pope Paul VI (1965) said: 'a wish borne in our heart for almost twenty centuries is being accomplished ... we are celebrating ... an opportunity to speak heart to heart with the whole world.'[7]

The Pope's vision of dialogue in support of a global culture of peace is rooted in a century of growing activism by religious leaders. Significant milestones include the World Parliament of Religions in

Chicago in 1893 and the peace plan of Pope Benedict XV in mid-World War I.

Arguably, this awakening of religious interest in questions of world organisation is attributable in part to the changing face of war in the 19th century. Powerful states were building standing armies, sometimes through conscription, and equipping them by means of an ever-growing military-industrial establishment. One of the main proposals laid before the First Vatican Council, convened in 1869, was to lend the authority of the Church to a strengthened Law of Nations, with particular reference to disarmament, arbitration, the redirecting of resources to the poor, and education for peace. Before this agenda for peace could be developed, the Franco-Prussian War led to the abrupt end of the Council (Araujo and Lucal, 2004, pp. 52–55). An analogous agenda for peace is central to the development of the Baha'i faith during the same period. In 1867 and 1868, Bahá'u'lláh addressed 'tablets' to kings and rulers urging them to establish a system of collective security, move towards disarmament, and show care and consideration for the rights of the poor.

In the 21st century, religious actors have continued to demonstrate a positive attitude towards the UN and the principle of global cooperation. This is reflected, for example, in faith-based initiatives in support of the UN SDGs (as mentioned in the Introduction) and human rights (Beirut Declaration, 2017).

But the question is, does the path of planetary awareness lead to a definite destination in terms of the future political organisation of the planet?

The Roman Empire with its Pax Romana offered a political vision that pointed in some respects towards the unity of peoples. But this unity was in practice extremely uneven in its effects and relied partly on severe coercion; for some perceptive writers of the time, unity based on Roman power and Roman state religion repeated many of the same damaging patterns of thought that characterised earlier national societies, only this time in the name of a much larger political entity.

Furthermore, it contradicts all the evidence of history to suppose that some revolution in our affairs will obviate the need for politics or exempt future generations from difficult acts of discernment.

Therefore, the right approach, we argue, is to work towards insights or axioms that are liberating in our present cultural context. We should think mainly in a medium-term perspective, laying down a path or throwing a bridge to the future. The goal is to prepare rather than pre-empt the choices to be made by the next generation.

There may be a useful distinction to be made between, on the one hand, the principle of a 'world political authority', and on the other hand, the practical objective of working towards a global 'civilisation' or 'common peace'. The difference between a 'world authority' and a 'common peace' resides partly in the difference between building an overarching political structure and nurturing the pre-political values out of which rules, programmes, budgets, and initiatives can be developed step by step.

We should aspire to moving gradually, by non-violent methods, from unexamined patterns of control and confrontation to conscious cooperation, from force-based structures to truth-based structures. Once this journey towards justice is underway, good will and friendship will take root. As a medium-term objective, we should work at the global level to transform habits and assumptions and create common reference points; but not – or not now – as a means to a single form of government on a planetary scale.

Global systemic change is already much discussed in relation to climate change. In that context, 2050 is mentioned as the date by which humanity needs to find a new direction. Our particular premise, that axioms of the historical imagination are an essential part of long-term diplomatic strategy, should be explored in the perspective of that time scale. To arrive at a better common understanding of the nature of effective action, and the role of religion in helping to enable effective action, will require multifaceted efforts over decades.

NOTES

1 Solzhenitsyn's speech can be found on the website of the Nobel Foundation at www.nobelprize.org.
2 This passage was drawn to our attention by Oswyn Murray.
3 We are grateful to Dirk Evers for an illuminating discussion of the connotations of this German word.
4 The Schuman Declaration is available on the website of the Robert Schuman Foundation at: www.robert-schuman.eu/en/declaration-of-9-may-1950.

5 Vegetius' *De Re Militari*.
6 In his 2006 speech to members of the Centesimus Annus Pro Pontifice Foundation, Clementine Hall, Friday 19 May; www.vatican.va.
7 In his address on 4 October 1965; https://w2.vatican.va/content/paul-vi/en/speeches/1965.index.html.

REFERENCES

Araujo, R.J. and Lucal, J.A. (2004). *Papal Diplomacy and the Quest for Peace: The Vatican and International Organisation from the Early Years to the League of Nations*. Ann Arbor, MI: Sapienta Press.

Aristotle. (1972 [1925]). *Nicomachean Ethics*, translated with an introduction by Sir David Ross. London: Oxford University Press.

Augustine. (1972). *City of God*, translated by H. Bettenson with an introduction by David Knowles. Harmondsworth: Penguin Books.

Benedict XVI. (2006). Speech to the Participants in the Meeting Sponsored by the Centesimus Annus Pro Pontifice Foundation, 19 May. www.vatican.va.

Camdessus, M. (2019). 'Faith in a Better World: Embracing the Mission to Shape the World of Tomorrow.' Address to the 7th Faith and Life Convention, Belfast, 27 September.

Chan, J. (2014). *Confucian Perfectionism: A Political Philosophy for Modern Times*. Princeton and Oxford: Princeton University Press.

Francis. (2016). Conferral of the Charlemagne Prize: Address of His Holiness Pope Francis, 6 May, Vatican. www.vatican.va.

Gandhi, R. (1999). *Revenge and Reconciliation: Understanding South Asian History*. New Delhi: Penguin Books India.

Harari, J.N. (2014). *Sapiens: A Brief History of Humankind*. London: Harvill Secker.

Heraclitus. (1957). In the Diels-Kranz ordering, in G.S. Kirk and J.E. Raven. *The Presocratic Philosophers*. Cambridge: Cambridge University Press.

Kirk, G.S. and Raven, J.E. (1957). *The Presocratic Philosophers*. Cambridge: Cambridge University Press.

Lane, M. (2014). *Greek and Roman Political Ideas*. London: Pelican.

Mandelbaum, M. (2019). *The Rise and Fall of Peace on Earth*. Oxford: Oxford University Press.

Office of the United Nations High Commissioner for Human Rights (OHCHR). (2017). 'The Beirut Declaration and Its 18 Commitments on "Faith for Rights".' www.ohchr.org.

Paul VI. (1965). 'Address to the United Nations Organisation,' 4 October. https://w2.vatican.va/content/paul-vi/en/speeches/1965.index.html.

Paul VI. (1972). 'Message for the World Day of Peace.' https://w2.vatican.va/content/paul-vi/en.

Philo of Alexandria. (1902). 'De Vita Mosis, Lib. I,' in L. Cohn (ed.), *Philonis Alexandrini Opera Quae Supersunt*, Vol. IV. Berlin: Reimer.

Plato. (1925). *Lysis, Symposium, Gorgias*, translated by W.R.M. Lamb. Loeb Classical Library. Cambridge: Harvard University Press.

Plutarch. (1936). *Moralia*, Vol. IV, including the essay 'On the Fortune or Virtue of Alexander,' translated by F.C. Babbitt. Loeb Classical Library. Cambridge: Harvard University Press.

Shelley, P. (2003). 'The Mask of Anarchy,' in Z. Leader and M. O'Neill (eds.), *Percy Bysshe Shelley: The Major Works*. Oxford: Oxford University Press.

Thapar, R. (1961). *Aśhoka and the Decline of the Mauryas*. Oxford: Oxford University Press.

Thapar, R. (2008). Humanities in a Globalising World. Speech on the Presentation of the 2008 Kluge Prize, Library of Congress.

Thucydides. (1996). *The Landmark Thucydides: A Comprehensive Guide to the Peloponnesian War* (revised edition of the R. Crawley translation), edited by R.B. Strassler. New York: Free Press.

Xenophon. (1998) *Cyropaedia: Bks. 1–4*, translated by W. Miller. Loeb Classical Library. Cambridge: Harvard University Press.

4

UNDERSTANDING HOW CHANGE HAPPENS

THE FACTORS THAT ACCOMPANY HEALING IN A WOUNDED SOCIAL STRUCTURE

As a young man with radical ideas, the poet Pushkin considered himself fortunate not to have been caught up in the Decembrist Revolution. Later, Pushkin saw a prophetic role for literature that works, not in the Decembrists' revolutionary way, by confrontation, but through a gradual cultural transformation. The following passage occurs in Pushkin's short novel *Kapitanskaya Dochka* (*The Captain's Daughter*; Pushkin, 1954 [1836], p. 66, translation slightly adapted):

> Young man, if these lines of mine ever fall into your hands, remember that the best and most enduring of changes are those which proceed from an improvement in morals and customs, and not from violent upheavals.

Pushkin's contemporary, Shelley, did not follow his friend Byron to war. Instead, he devoted the last year of his short life to his *Defence of Poetry* (discussed in Chapter 1) and his *Philosophical View of Reform*. Shelley did not rule out 'insurrection' as a last resort. His goal, however, was to develop a strategy of gradual change through non-violence. Gandhi would quote Shelley's (2003c) 'Mask of Anarchy' at public meetings.

W. B. Yeats, in his poem 'To a Shade', compares the statesman Parnell to Sir Hugh Lane, who wanted to establish a gallery of impressionist paintings in Dublin (Yeats, 1994). The gallery project is seen by Yeats as an investment in future generations' receptiveness to ideas – their 'loftier thought' and 'sweeter emotion'. These terms echo the *chuvstva dobroie* ('nobler feelings') in a poem in which Pushkin (2008, p. 123) compares the reception of his own work within Russian society, and its transformative effect, to the impact of the Alexander Column that had recently been unveiled in front of the Winter Palace. Yeats intended the revival of Irish culture through the Abbey Theatre to accompany a political awakening, exactly as Pushkin or Shelley would have recommended.

In the last paragraph of *Crime and Punishment*, Dostoevsky (2000) refers to 'a man's gradual rebirth, his gradual crossing from one world to another, his acquaintance with a new, as yet unknown reality'. Our third axiom, that *we should identify and explore the factors that accompany healing in a wounded social structure*, proceeds from the poets' vision of how benign change happens. We can translate Dostoevsky's conception of a gradual crossing from one world to another to the domain of society and civilisation. The factors that accompany healing in a wounded social structure can then be identified and understood.

Crime and Punishment 'teaches reality and justice' in the face of 'revolutionary frenzy' (to borrow phrases from Yeats's 1923 Nobel lecture, 'The Bounty of Sweden'). The story unfolds in the slums of St Petersburg in the burning July heat. We encounter hellish living conditions, the near impossibility of ordinary family life. One of the main consequences of extreme poverty is prostitution. Throughout the novel, we learn a great deal about wages, rents, and prices, and how these affect the lives of the characters: not even *Ulysses* has as much detailed information on the cost of living as *Crime and Punishment*.

The names of the main characters in *Crime and Punishment* tell us a great deal about Dostoevsky's vision of non-violent social change. 'Raskolnikov' comes from a verb associated with splitting wood and also with breakaway movements in the Church – unpleasant associations. Raskolnikov's good and loyal friend is Razumikhin, suggesting 'razum', meaning reason and intellect. The prostitute whose heart becomes a 'fountain of life' for Raskolnikov is Sonya; the full form of her name is Sofya, from the Greek 'Sophia', which is the biblical term for the 'divine wisdom'. The drama of the novel – divisiveness and violence versus the transformative power of reason and charity – is summarised in the play of names.

Two aspects of Raskolnikov's character are of particular interest in the light of the approach we take in this book. The first is the absence in his life of a father figure or any other form of benign authority. Raskolnikov lost his father at a young age – just as Prince Myshkin, the 'idiot', is an orphan, there are fatherless young men in *Demons*, and the father of the Karamazov brothers had abdicated the role of parent. Sonya loves her father; but he, Marmeladov, is completely unable to provide for his children. Dostoevsky's main characters have no one to look up to and trust; broken family structures are mirrored by the pitilessness of economic and political structures.

Second, in the character of Raskolnikov, a key 19th-century political idea is examined close-up: that the 'great' man needs to set aside the 'ordinary' man's understanding of morality. The proposition that some agents are above ordinary morality contributed to what actually happened in Soviet Russia. The dream of a perfect society to be achieved by a small, ruthless avant-garde brought about a murderous dictatorship whose victims are counted in the millions.

What is less well understood is that Dostoevsky foresaw not only the risk of totalitarianism but also a threat to the increasingly open and secular societies that he knew from his travels in Western Europe. At the beginning of *Crime and Punishment*, Raskolnikov believes, or almost believes, that a successful human being is someone who overcomes his inhibitions and relies on skill to play the great role that he imagines for himself. A 'technocratic paradigm' (to borrow a phrase from Pope Francis) begins to shape an ethical vision – and this, according to Dostoevsky, underlies the danger faced by both Russia and Western Europe.

Raskolnikov's 'gradual crossing from one world to another' begins with his encounter with Sonya. Sonya's relationship with Raskolnikov unfolds through time according to an unpredictable pattern. In the end, Raskolnikov expresses his love for Sonya through the gesture of falling at her feet. He cannot find words for what is happening. The stages by which healing occurs do not lend themselves to exact measurement.

The believer Sonya intuits what is good in Raskolnikov, though she cannot follow his thinking; while Raskolnikov, not a believer, comes to respect and value the religious aspect of Sonya's life. Dostoevsky wrote four major novels on his return to St Petersburg from prison and exile – *Crime and Punishment, The Idiot, Demons* (or *The Possessed*), and *The Brothers Karamazov*. Together, the novels explore the intersection of politics and religion with life as lived and experienced. Does the relationship between Sonya and Raskolnikov hint at how the respectful engagement of public authorities with religious belief can bring new energy to the global conversation? A crucial aspect of the relationship between Raskolnikov and Sonya is that it is real and fruitful, though difficult to define. Previously, Raskolnikov was in the opposite situation. His clear and original ideas led to a brilliant article for the *Periodical Review*; in practice, he misjudged his own deepest instincts. Raskolnikov and Sonya together discover hope.

In the light of Dostoevsky's conception of a gradual crossing from one world to another, we attempt in what follows to describe the anatomy of benign social change – the factors that accompany healing in a wounded social structure.

A COMPOSITION WITH TEN PANELS

Our argument in relation to these principles or indicators of benign change does not follow a forensic logic. We look on the ten themes pursued below as panels in a broad composition, like a chapel by Giotto, Signorelli, or Michelozzo in which separate images are interrelated and mutually supportive. In this composition, the reader is invited into a 'conversation'. Whether for him or her there is an emerging, convincing pattern depends on a continuing process of reflection. 'Viewers' of this chapter are invited to add brighter colours to our images or to enlarge our 'composition' with new panels.

We assert that effective, non-violent action in the service of justice is marked, by and large, by the following characteristics:

1. mercy
2. dharma, decorum, religious reverence
3. respect for nature
4. the virtue of hesitation
5. humility as the primordial human value
6. gratuitousness and generosity

7. knowledge of the particular situation combined with a vision of the whole
8. gradualness
9. finding unity in the presence of difference
10. constructive engagement with the holders of power

What all these ten themes have in common is that embracing them requires a certain style of imagination – call it the religious, literary, or historical imagination. We can acquire a deeper perspective on the nature of social change and therefore on the efficacy of different forms of political and diplomatic action.

MERCY

None of our factors of benign change involves action based primarily on self-interest or technical proficiency. On the contrary, they are more like dimensions of Shakespeare's quality of mercy:

> The quality of mercy is not strained;
> It droppeth as the gentle rain from heaven
> Upon the place beneath. It is twice blest;
> It blesseth him that gives and him that takes ...
> It is enthronèd in the hearts of kings,
> It is an attribute to God himself.
> *(Merchant of Venice*, Act 4, Scene 1, lines 190–196)

Shakespeare is in no doubt that mercy as a political value arises from the religious perspective:

> we do pray for mercy;
> And that same prayer doth teach us all to render
> The deeds of mercy.

Psalm 85 (Vulgate 84) is a prayer for peace:

> Mercy and Truth have come together,
> Justice and Peace have embraced.
> Truth raised its arms from the earth,
> And Justice bent down from heaven.

The image of truth raising its arms and justice bending down from heaven suggests a child and its parents. The children in this picture, that is, human beings, should respect truth and practise mercy.

Hebrew words such as *hēsed* ('loving kindness and equity') and *tsedakah* ('justice-with-mercy') imply that our judgement of a situation is not even true or accurate in the absence of a saving or protective instinct that works in favour of the vulnerable.

DHARMA, DECORUM, RELIGIOUS REVERENCE

The great world civilisations have cherished a perspective in which decorum, tolerance, and religious reverence act as a check on personal self-aggrandisement, especially by rulers. In ancient China, the observance of rites and rituals (*li*) is a key to the good of society. Laws and magistracies are for the benefit of the people, not the rulers. This benign dispensation is under the protection of Heaven: 'The people are of supreme importance; the altars to the gods of earth and grain come next; last comes the ruler' (Mencius 7B.14, quoted by Chan, 2014, p. 29).

In Ashoka's Rock Edicts, dharma, a way of life in conformity with truth, is a new and unifying concept. The shared social meaning promoted by Ashoka respects religion while not imposing a single religious doctrine. To live in accordance with dharma implies religious literacy and a moral disposition to respect limits.

Even in late 5th-century Athens, with traditional Greek religion under challenge, the first clause of the most important peace treaty of the era (the Peace of Nikias) reads as follows (Thucydides, 1996, V.18):

> With regard to the Panhellenic temples, everyone who wishes, according to the customs of his country, to sacrifice in them, to travel to them, to consult the oracles, or to attend the games, shall be guaranteed security in doing so, both by sea and by land.

This concern with sanctuaries and rituals implies the presence of a pre-political culture, and also that a religious outlook disposes us to obey social rules for reasons that go beyond self-interest. In the Funeral Oration, Pericles praises the obedience of his fellow citizens to 'unwritten law' (Thucydides, 1996, II.37.3).

'Wonders are many and none more wonderful than man', proclaims the chorus in the central ode of Sophocles' *Antigone*. This hymn to human potential ends with an affirmation of the part played by the 'laws of the earth' and religious reverence in enabling humanity to flourish (*Antigone*, pp. 368–370): 'When we respect the laws of the earth and the sworn justice of the gods,[1] the polis is exalted.'

Explaining her stand, Antigone invokes the same concept as Pericles: the 'unwritten laws (*agrapta nomima*) whose life is not of today and yesterday but forever' (*Antigone*, pp. 454–457).

RESPECT FOR NATURE

The following are short excerpts from Ecclesiasticus 43:

> The sun, as he emerges, proclaims at his rising
> 'A thing of wonder is the work of the Most-High!'
> Great is the Lord who made him ...
> The beauty of the heavens, the glory of the stars,
> The Lord's glittering world so far above!
> They take position according to his words and his decision ...
> See the rainbow and praise its maker ...
> Ice forms,
> And water puts it on like a breastplate ...
> Many things even greater than these are hidden,
> For we have seen only a few of his works.

In a religious perspective, there is more to nature and the world than what we measure scientifically. There is a depth, a purpose, and a beauty that is not ours to give or take away. 'There lives the dearest freshness deep down things', writes the poet Gerard Manley Hopkins (2005, p. 1166) in 'God's Grandeur': the world is good and deserves from us the response of wonder. The Shinto religion in Japan is based on a reverence for nature.

To accept, even as a working hypothesis, that the earth and its creatures are in some sense 'given' or sacred, has ethical implications going beyond the sense of decorum or reverence that disposes us to live under laws. In the first instance, a sense of the 'given-ness' of life can have a particular impact on our approach to environmental questions:

> It is impossible to see any way out of this crisis without an acceptance of limits and limitations, and this in turn, is, I think, intimately related to the idea of the sacred, however one may wish to conceive of it.
>
> (Ghosh, 2016, p. 215)

THE VIRTUE OF HESITATION

'Religious reverence' is relevant in many other sets of circumstances. Our spontaneous wonder or shame or anger in the face of gross facts is often more affecting than acute legal reasoning in preparing us for the work of justice. 'Cruel and unusual punishment', a criterion based on a personal sense of measure, is forbidden under law. Similarly, the concept of 'reasonable accommodation', again depending on our sense of measure, is used in many situations, for example, to ensure equal rights to persons with disabilities.

Socrates spoke of the intervention of his *daimonion*, a spirit not of his own making that holds him back from certain courses of action. In Thucydides, a far-seeing hesitation (*mellēsis promēthēs*) is a centrally important value closely related to divine law (*theios nomos*), religious reverence (*eusebeia*), the sacred (*to hosion*), and the shared laws that offer hope to all (*koinoi nomoi*).[2]

The disastrous Sicilian Expedition is central to the structure of Thucydides' history. In the debate at Athens, the 'far-seeing hesitation' of which Nikias is capable is overruled by the Assembly. The *daimonion* of Socrates prompts a value judgement that coincides exactly on this particular point with the thinking of Nikias and Thucydides (Plutarch, *Life of Nikias*, XIII.6): 'Socrates' daimonion indicated plainly that the expedition would make for the ruin of Athens.'

Today, dealing with emerging issues in such fields as AI, biophysics, and new weaponry (cyber; lethal autonomous weapons systems), we may lose our way if we rely only on discursive reasoning. There are circumstances in which the sheer 'enormity' of what is proposed, the abandonment of a human scale, should give us pause.

The Greek virtue of hesitation, or compunction, partly anticipates the *Heuristik der Furcht* ('heuristics of fear') developed in the 20th century by Hans Jonas. For Jonas, an appropriate hesitation in exploiting technology accompanies a heightened sense of planetary awareness. There should be no disconnect between individual moral choices and the sustainability of life on the planet (Jonas, 1984).

HUMILITY AS THE PRIMORDIAL HUMAN VALUE

We (most of us) sense that humility should govern our approach to nature. The world around us is the extraordinary result of billions of years of evolution. What does it mean to destroy some of its most beautiful features in the equivalent of an instant? To appreciate the enormity of what is happening is to begin to acquire humility. By humility, we also mean the question of Jesus (Matthew 7:4): 'How can you say to your brother, "Brother, let me take the speck out of your eye," when you yourself fail to see the plank in your own eye?' To the degree that we are willing to examine our current assumptions, we will embrace a humbler and more 'dialogical' approach to international relations.

Do we have the humility to hope? To accept that something new and better can happen in history, even when we ourselves do not see the full picture? The shepherds in St Luke's Gospel exemplify political humility. Moses and David are shepherds. Greek and Roman poets portray themselves as shepherds or goatherds. In their closeness to the natural world, their cooperative work patterns, their love of song, their sense of fairness, and their openness to new things, the shepherds of ancient literature embody the best of 'indigenous' culture; they represent, before we can put it into words, the religious, ethical, and political literacy that lies at the heart of our objectives in putting together this book.

An important dimension to 'religious reverence' and humility as political values is the light they shed on the relationship between act and consequence.

We read in Psalm 127 (Vulgate 126), verse 1:

> Unless the Lord builds the house,
> Those who build it labour in vain;
> Unless the Lord watches over the city,
> The watchman stays awake in vain.

Psalm 85 (Vulgate 84), quoted earlier on, calls on us to raise our arms like children to ask for justice. The Psalm continues (verse 12):

> The Lord bestows happiness
> As the soil gives its harvest.

In these passages, peace is an after-phenomenon, a gift from God. The Psalms give us an explicitly religious perspective on history; but even in the eyes of secular historians and political scientists, it is often difficult to prove a direct causal connection between one event and another.

Military theorists sometimes explain the use of force as a way of 'sending a message'. However, the broader the geographical canvas and the longer the historical time scale, the harder it becomes to establish how and where the message has been received or to assess 'proportionality'. In the course of events, multiple short-term and long-term factors mingle with ordinary human fallibility. Some 'messages' turn events in unexpected directions. In his account of the slide to war in July 1914, the British historian Christopher Clark (2013, p. 555) states, '[A] profound sundering of ethical and political perspectives eroded consensus and sapped trust'.

As in systems theory, there is always a bigger picture in politics; often there is a feedback loop through which the source of change is itself transformed along the way. Military action is among the least precise of instruments. It can sow the seeds of future chaos; by a ricochet effect, it can impact negatively on the clear-sightedness of the doer.

The virtue of hope, to which we turn later, belongs in the space of uncertainty that separates our actions from their outcome; and in the space between our seeming powerlessness and our strong sense of what is right. 'We treat, God heals' – this insight in Ayurveda is often applicable in a political situation.

GRATUITOUSNESS AND GENEROSITY

The T'ang poet Bai Juyi (or 'Po-Chü-I') is celebrated for his sense of social justice and for the tension he experiences between his role as a high official and his love of everyday things. To find release, Bai Juyi puts the 'confusion' of the capital and the competition for 'fame' and 'profit' as far out of his mind as possible. In the autumn of 816, when in his 40s, Bai Juyi builds a chapel for himself and his friends high on a mountainside close by a Buddhist temple (Levy, 1971, pp. 54–55, slightly adapted):

> How shall I wash my ears?
> With the falling stream flying above my roof.
> How shall I wash my eyes?
> With white lotuses ...
> In my left hand, I hold a single jug,

In my right hand grasp a five-stringed lute ...
Drunk on desire, I look to heaven and sing ...
A man of the fields
Mistakenly drawn into the net of the world
Returns to the mountains,
A weary bird returns to thick foliage,
A deadened fish comes back to the clear stream.

Here is a passage from Seneca, the Stoic philosopher who served for many years as the Emperor Nero's principal political advisor (1935, *De Beneficiis* I.1.9):

the immortal gods, though some men neglect them or are irreligious, continue to shower their benefits upon us; for they act according to their divine nature and help all alike, even those who fail to understand their generosity.

Seneca questions whether we can explain a close and trusting relationship between doctor and patient in terms of the size of the doctor's fee. If the gods give us their benefits freely, it follows, for Seneca, that we too must give freely.

Here is a passage from Al-Insan, the 76th chapter of the Quran:

And they give food, despite their love of it, to the needy, and the orphan and the prisoner. 'We feed you only for the sake of God. We do not desire any reward from you, nor any thanks.'

Bai Juyi, with his interest in Buddhism; Seneca, as a Stoic; and of course the Quran, all have a religious perspective. However, as regards gratuitousness as a personal and political value, there is perhaps no clear borderline between the best of religious and the best of philosophical thought. In Chapter 3, we discussed Aristotle's thesis that our pursuit of a common project tends as a matter of experience to turn into friendship (*philia*) and ways of interacting that are no longer selfishly calculating. The culminating insight of Aristotle's ethics is that we pursue virtue for its own sake, and 'happiness comes afterwards' (*epiginomenon ti*). Aristotle's word for happiness, *eudaimonia*, comes from the word *daimon*, and implies, like the *daimonion* of Socrates, a god given state that we cannot manufacture or control.

KNOWLEDGE OF THE PARTICULAR SITUATION
COMBINED WITH A VISION OF THE WHOLE

Our first axiom is focused on the discernment of reality. Our second axiom concerns the 'imaging' or visualising of peace. These two factors in benign change – knowledge of the particular and a vision of the whole – are interconnected.

In the Irish context, John Hume used to argue that a common factor connects the truth of the situation in Northern Ireland to the values underlying the European project. The big picture in Europe makes it easier to deal with the particular challenge in Northern Ireland. A local peace process can anticipate or reflect a broader trend. The whole is greater than the sum of its parts.

The principle that the 'micro' and the 'macro' can mirror one another has deep implications that go to the heart of our vision in this book: something that they have in common links all situations in which justice and hope are at stake. We have an urgent need, as the 21st century advances, to visualise a 'counterpart' at the global level to the processes we want to see happen in the Middle East, the Korean peninsula, the Indian subcontinent, and other situations of actual or potential conflict. In a culturally integrated world, a vacuum of values at the 'macro' level impacts on the prospects for peace in each individual context.

GRADUALNESS

In situations of conflict, we generally try to put in place a process that sets events on a new trajectory. In Northern Ireland, the Good Friday Agreement (Belfast Agreement) of 1998[3] is the outcome of a peace process that lasted in one form or another for a quarter-century. The implementation of the Agreement over the last 20 and more years is also best understood as a process. 'Gradualness' of this kind belongs among the principles of benign change. Working to ensure that time is on our side is a key value in the context of our sixth and last axiom concerning the 'frameworks of engagement' that make multilateralism fit for purpose.

The gradual processes we have in mind are often open-ended. There are steps valid in themselves – intrinsically valid – whose precise consequences cannot be measured or foreseen.

FINDING UNITY IN THE PRESENCE OF DIFFERENCE

'A process, not the victory of a single point of view' – implicit in this common reading of the accommodation reached in Northern Ireland is that the anatomy of any benign transformation includes respect for difference. 'Parity of esteem' means more than coexistence; it is intended to lead to common action. 'Spilling our sweat' (the often repeated saying of John Hume) in the common interest brings a new perspective to questions of identity, ethos, and aspiration.

'Finding unity in the presence of difference' is a condition of both democratic politics and international negotiations. According to the traditions of liberal democracy, a government should be in a position to rely on the loyalty of the opposition ('Her Majesty's Loyal Opposition', as the British say). Diplomacy entails accepting the legitimacy of our negotiating partners. We are out, not to destroy the other side, but to build relationships and move forward together.

Achieving unity-in-difference reflects a truth about human nature. Virtue is outward-looking – not a matter of 'irreducible identity' so much as an acquired disposition to which we give expression when interacting with others. Unity of purpose does not eliminate differences; on the contrary, a culture of encounter sustained through time amounts in itself to unity of purpose. 'Unity in the presence of difference' better describes a functioning political compromise than the sophistic notion that a single product is being cleverly sold in different ways to different constituencies.

In the 21st century, accelerating change often translates into a dangerous incapacity: we no longer seem to grasp that the encounter of different points of view, if conducted fairly, helps us journey together into the future and is, in itself, a form of solidarity. What needs to be recaptured is a sense of the intimate connection between respecting other people in their diversity and deepest humanity, preparing ourselves for dialogue and encounter, and gradually shaping a world characterised by an awareness of the oneness of humanity and the responsibility of each person to contribute to the collective well-being of the human race. The European Enlightenment looked forward to 'an age of reason'; the 'Axial Age' to which we look forward in this book is 'an age of sharing'.

CONSTRUCTIVE ENGAGEMENT WITH THE HOLDERS
OF POWER: A BIBLICAL REFLECTION

The factors that accompany healing in a wounded social structure are clearly signposted in the Bible, including the need to engage constructively, or to be available to engage constructively, with those who hold power.

The movement initiated by two cousins – John the Baptist and Jesus – makes use of at least two key political concepts, 'assembly of the people' (*ekklēsia*) and 'choice of a common life' (*koinōnia*). This development of existing thought patterns changes the focus of our attention in significant ways.

> You are Peter and on this Rock, I will build my *ekklēsia*.
>
> (Matthew 16:18)

In Greek political thought, the term *ekklēsia* is associated with 'popular' or people's power. Its use here can be taken to imply that change has many of its roots at the base of society. A new lifestyle and outlook among ordinary people, based on new forms of association, can transform the lived experience of those who persevere and suffer, and influence, over time, those who hold political, economic, and social power.

In the New Testament, that other Greek political term *koinōnia*, which we translate as 'the choice of a common life', is used to describe the shared life among followers of the new 'way':

> If the shared life of the Spirit (*koinōnia pneumatos*) means anything ...
>
> (Philippians 2:1)

> If we live our lives in the light, as he is in the light, we have a shared life together (*koinōnia*).
>
> (1 John 1:7)

In a passage to which we will return in Chapter 5, St Paul describes himself as the *koinōnos* of both the slave-owner Philemon and the slave Onesimus; he is 'in communion with' both (Letter to Philemon, verse 17).

Are John and Jesus thinking politically? The character of Roman governance is at issue throughout the gospel story, from the census at Bethlehem to the probing of Jesus on the taxation question to the executions on Golgotha.

Jesus, following in the footsteps of the prophets, proclaims that the conglomerate of interests that dominates first century Palestine – the prevailing 'system' – should be questioned in the light of the 'kingdom of God'. To accept the baptism of John, means, among other things, to live and act in accordance with a social vision rooted in reality; it means attending to what is unattended to in the standard opinions of the time.

The Letter of James is written in Jerusalem not many years after the death of Jesus. 'James the Just' was respected in the community, as we see in Josephus (2006, 20.9), and he was a leader among the followers of the 'way' of Jesus. A strong political imagination echoes throughout the letter:

> Be doers of the word (*poiētai logou*, 1: 22) ... Pure, untainted religion in the eyes of God our Father is this: to watch over orphans and widows in their affliction. (1:27)

The author is scathing about status differences:

> Now suppose a man comes into your synagogue, beautifully dressed and with a gold ring on, and at the same time, a poor man comes in in shabby clothes. (2:2)

To treat the rich and the poor differently is to contradict the 'law of freedom' (2:12), which demands that we judge the world (4:4) in the light of an independent God-given standard.

How, then, might we characterise the political imagination of John, Jesus, and James? Jesus states that 'the weightier part of the law is discernment, mercy, and faith' (Matthew 23:23).

Mercy (*eleos*) – 'our being moved by suffering' – draws us into a differently imagined social space. St Paul, in the passage from Philippians just quoted, identifies a 'deep-felt mercy' as a principal characteristic of those who embrace the new form of shared life. The gift of discernment (*krisis*) invites us to analyse the space that we share with others in terms of policy alternatives. Faith (Greek *pistis*; Latin, *fides*) is not altogether different to what Cicero means by 'good faith' – a willingness to trust in an unseen truth that may or may not be reflected in the civil law.

John and Jesus, like James, are careful not to mobilise politically against the Roman system; they are not oppositional (*antitassomenoi*) in the sense described in St Paul's Letter to the Romans (13:2).

Nevertheless, we are informed (Mark 6:20) that Herod Antipas 'liked listening' to his prisoner John the Baptist. Pilate starts a dialogue with Jesus before being swept back into the Roman official's familiar world of political calculation. On the Areopagus and on several other occasions, St Paul explains his thinking in a public or official setting.

John is put to death for no clear legal reason, but as a favour to Herodias's daughter. Jesus is executed, not for an identifiable political offence, but apparently because claims he has made about his identity, and does not deny, are perceived by Pilate as somehow disorderly in themselves; a prefect had power to suppress dissent ('contumacy'), even where no crime had been committed. Josephus can see no legal basis for the execution of either John or James (2006, 18.116, 20.9).

FROM ANTIGONE TO KEN SARO-WIWA

To breathe life into the ten factors of peaceful transformation, nothing is more important than the role of the courageous individual who perceives the underlying truth of situations and brings this to attention. Like Antigone, such individuals often lack the protection of established religious authorities. Like Antigone, they are often the victims of a legal rigmarole that is not law. To conclude the present chapter, we offer a contemporary case study. Ken Saro-Wiwa separated truth from falsehood and took a stand for justice in the face of seemingly invincible social forces.

'LORD TAKE MY SOUL, BUT THE STRUGGLE CONTINUES': KEN SARO-WIWA AND THE OGONI CAUSE – BY CIARA JOYCE

What motivates an individual to make the ultimate sacrifice to right a perceived injustice? To subject themselves to physical and personal hardships, to be separated from their family and friends and face financial ruin for the sake of others? The case of Ken Saro-Wiwa, the Nigerian writer and activist, and the Ogoni Nine is well known to those with an interest in human rights. On 10 November 1995, Saro-Wiwa and eight of his colleagues were executed by the

Nigerian government. The crime they were found guilty of was incitement to murder. Brought before a military tribunal during the dictatorship of Sani Abacha, the trial was a farce and a guilty verdict was predetermined.

Ogoni, one of the River States on the coast of Nigeria and home to a population of over half a million people, came to international attention following the campaign to save it from environmental devastation due to the extraction of oil by Royal Dutch Shell. Despite the huge profits made by Shell and the Nigerian Government from the oil rich Niger Delta, Ogoni lacked basic facilities, such as running water and reliable electricity. Pollution caused by the oil industry had a devastating effect on a community dependent on fishing and farming for its livelihood. It also had a negative impact on the health of the community.

In 1990, Saro-Wiwa established the Movement for the Survival of the Ogoni People (MOSOP) and began a peaceful campaign to highlight these issues and bring Shell to account for the damage caused. Although they led a non-violent campaign for change, Saro-Wiwa and his colleagues were arrested in May 1994. Four Ogoni chiefs were murdered during a night of violence in the region, and the MOSOP activists were charged with 'procuring and inciting' others to murder. Despite an international campaign to save their lives, including a Nobel Peace Prize nomination for Saro-Wiwa, the Ogoni Nine were executed.

Saro-Wiwa was a successful businessman, a writer of novels, poetry, and children's books. A complex individual, he was a man of conscience, charismatic and contradictory, and described as generous to a fault by his eldest son, Ken Wiwa (2000, p. 21). An agnostic for most of his adult life, Saro-Wiwa's motivation seems to come from a deep loyalty to his people – the Ogoni; all his personal success, he maintained, was for them. Compelled by a belief in justice and human rights for a people he knew had been deeply wronged, he put his personal resources and his own freedom to the forefront in order to free the Ogoni – the people and land, which he believed to be one – from continued exploitation and destruction. There was no personal gain for Saro-Wiwa, apart from the peace of mind that resulted from yielding to his sense of duty and seeing the growth of a movement he founded.

We are fortunate that, as a prolific writer, Saro-Wiwa captured his thoughts and aspirations for the Ogoni on paper. During his time in military detention Saro-Wiwa corresponded widely, including with an Irish nun, Sister Majella McCarron, who is a member of the Missionary Sisters of Our Lady of the Apostles (OLA). His letters were smuggled out of military detention in breadbaskets and donated to Maynooth University library in 2011. From his letters and his writing, Saro-Wiwa could only be described as a man devoted to the Ogoni – people, landscape and culture – and as a man resigned to his fate. In December 1994, he wrote to his son Ken Wiwa: 'I am a protector of the Ogoni' (Wiwa, 2000, p. 167). Ken Wiwa also felt that it pained his father that an area like Ogoni, rich in resources, was one of the 'poorest corners of Africa' (Wiwa, 2000, p. 81).

During his confinement, Saro-Wiwa found comfort in reading both the Bible and the Quran. Ken Wiwa described him as 'at peace with himself' (Wiwa, 2000, p. 211). In his letters to Sister Majella, Saro-Wiwa expresses his hopes for the Ogoni and the future of the campaign, while reflecting on the possible outcome of his incarceration. On 13 July 1994, he writes,

> there are a lot more difficulties ahead. However, I believe that I've done what God wanted me to, and have spared nothing to achieve his will. He will have to decide what happens to me. Incarceration is nothing. I must expect more of it, and even death. But I do want to live to help re-create Ogoni society.
>
> (Archive, PP/7/3)

On 21 March 1995, he writes,

> I have never really felt I was in danger. The sure knowledge of my innocence gave me that feeling. I thought that I'd remain in captivity until God should have used that fact to make the Ogoni cause better known and pave the way for solving some of the many problems which confront the Ogoni people and similar groups in Nigeria, if not the African continent. Big thought. Big assignment.
>
> (Archive, PP/7/23)

Saro-Wiwa is probably best understood by the words of the final statement he prepared but was prevented from reading at his trial:

I am a man of peace, of ideas. Appalled by the denigrating poverty of my people who live on a richly endowed land, distressed by their political marginalization and economic strangulation, angered by the devastation of their land, their ultimate heritage, anxious to preserve their right to life and to a decent living, and determined to usher to this country as a whole a fair and just democratic system which protects everyone and every ethnic group and gives us all a valid claim to human civilization, I have devoted my intellectual and material resources, my very life, to a cause in which I have total belief and from which I cannot be blackmailed or intimidated ... I call upon the Ogoni people, the peoples of the Niger Delta, and the oppressed ethnic minorities of Nigeria to stand up now and fight fearlessly and peacefully for their rights. History is on their side. God is on their side.

(Saro-Wiwa, 2005, p. 193)

With a clear mind and conscience, Saro-Wiwa appears to have kept his dedication and his focus until the very end. His reputed last words at the gallows, spoken in his native Khana, were 'Lord take my soul, but the struggle continues' (Wiwa, 2000, p. 218).

NOTES

1 *theōn t'enorkon dikān* – our translation.
2 III.82.4, III.82.6, III.82.8, III.84.2, III.84.3 – our translations.
3 Department of Foreign Affairs and Trade. (2018). The Good Friday agreement and today. www.dfa.ie/our-role-policies/northern-ireland/the-good-friday-agreement-and-today/.

REFERENCES

Baumgarth, W., and Regan, R. (eds.). (1988). *St. Thomas Aquinas on Law, Morality, and Politics*. Cambridge: Hackett Publishing Company.

Chan, J. (2014). *Confucian Perfectionism: A Political Philosophy for Modern Times*. Princeton and Oxford: Princeton University Press.

Clark, C. (2013). *The Sleepwalkers: How Europe Went to War in 1914*. London: Penguin Books.

Dostoevsky, F. (2000). *Crime and Punishment*, translated by C. Garnett, Ware: Wordsworth Editions.

Dostoevsky, F. (2003). *The Brothers Karamazov*, translated with and introduction and notes by D. McDuff (revised edition). London: Penguin Books.

Dostoevsky, F. (2004). *The Idiot*, translated with notes by D. McDuff. London: Penguin Books.

Dostoevsky, F. (2008). *Demons*, translated by R.A. Maguire. London: Penguin Books.

Finley, M. (1980). *Ancient Slavery and Modern Ideology*. London: Chatto and Windus.

Garnsey, P. (1996). *Ideas of Slavery from Aristotle to Augustine*. Cambridge: Cambridge University Press.

Ghosh, A. (2016). *The Great Derangement*. Gurgaon: Allen Lane.

Griffin, M. (1976). *Seneca: A Philosopher in Politics*. Oxford: Oxford University Press.

Hopkins, G.M. (2005). 'God's Grandeur,' in A.M. Eastman et al. (eds.), *The Norton Anthology of Poetry*, 5th edn., pp. 887–888. New York: W.W. Norton and Company.

Jonas, H. (1984). *The Imperative of Responsibility: In Search of an Ethics for the Technological Age*. Chicago: University of Chicago Press.

Josephus. (2006). *Jewish Antiquities*, translated by W. Whiston. Ware: Wordsworth Editions. (Whiston's translation was first published in 1737)

Ken Saro-Wiwa Archive, Maynooth University Library. PP/7/3. The letters written by Saro-Wiwa to Sister Majella McCarron are available for consultation at Maynooth University Library.

Levy, H. (1971). *Translations from Po-Chü-I's Collected Works*. New York: Paragon Book Reprint Corp.

Plutarch. (1916). *Pericles and Fabius Maximus, Nicias and Crassus*, translated by B. Perrin. Loeb Classical Library. Cambridge: Harvard University Press.

Pushkin, A.S. (1954). *The Captain's Daughter*, translated by Ivy and T. Litvinov. Moscow: Foreign Languages Publishing House (first published in Russian in 1836).

Pushkin, A.S. (2008). 'Untitled Poem,' in I.G. Irskaya and Y.G. Fridstein (eds.), *Alexander Pushkin: In Hopes of Fame and Bliss to Come*. Moscow: Bagrius (bilingual edition of Pushkin's selected poems).

Saro-Wiwa, K. (2005). *A Month and a Day and Letters*. Banbury, Oxford: Ayebia Clarke Publishing.

Seneca. (1935). *Moral Essays*, Volume III (De Beneficiis), translated by J.W. Basore. Loeb Classical Library. Cambridge: Harvard University Press.

Shelley, P. (2003a). 'A Defence of Poetry,' in Z. Leader and M. O'Neill (eds.), *Percy Bysshe Shelley: The Major Works*, pp. 674–701. Oxford: Oxford University Press.

Shelley, P. (2003b). 'A Philosophical View of Reform,' in Z. Leader and M. O'Neill (eds.), *Percy Bysshe Shelley: The Major Works*, pp. 636–674. Oxford: Oxford University Press.

Shelley, P. (2003c). 'The Mask of Anarchy,' in Z. Leader and M. O'Neill (eds.), *Percy Bysshe Shelley: The Major Works*. Oxford: Oxford University Press.

Sophocles. (1987). *Antigone*, edited with translation and notes by A. Brown. Warminster: Aris and Phillips.

Thucydides. (1996). *The Landmark Thucydides: A Comprehensive Guide to the Peloponnesian War* (revised edition of the Richard Crawley translation), edited by R.B. Strassler. New York: Free Press.

Wiwa, K. (2000). *In the Shadow of a Saint*. London: Doubleday.

Yeats, W. (1994). 'To a Shade', in B. Kiely (ed.), *Yeats' Ireland: An Illustrated Anthology*. London: Tiger Books International.

5

THE DIPLOMACY OF THE
TWO STANDARDS

THE NATURE OF POLITICAL ACTION

Our fourth axiom is that *the starting position for political deliberation is inevitably non-ideal*. We act always under constraint. What cannot be pictured now can become possible, given the right intermediate steps. Our fifth axiom, conceived against this background, is that *discernment in the midst of opacity in accordance with a common standard should become a core value in the conduct of international relations*. Our axioms are congruent with Amartya Sen's (2010) idea of justice. Sen calls for 'ways of judging how to reduce injustice and advance justice', even when we find it difficult to characterise 'a perfectly just arrangement' (Sen, 2010, pp. ix, 21). Whether at the global level or within nation states, 'a perfectly just arrangement' is beyond our reach, all the more so at a time of rapid change. Our axioms are also congruent with the relation between the 'Small Tranquillity' and 'Grand Union' in the Confucian worldview (Chan, 2014, p. 9). In discerning a way forward under unfavourable conditions, we accept lesser measures reflecting a lesser ideal (the Small Tranquillity) while keeping a higher vision (the Grand Union) in play as a guiding standard or 'regulative ideal'.

OUR FOURTH AXIOM: THE STARTING POSITION FOR POLITICAL DELIBERATION

BEING MORE: POLITICS AS TRANSITION

As a matter of experience, and in many religions as a matter of doctrine, any political dispensation is flawed and capable of improvement. Legitimacy does not mean perfection. Development – being more – is always a dimension of personal and public life. The practice of politics is a journey from an inherited situation, which in the nature of things is defective or deficient, towards a more just order. The concept of a 'just transition' underlies the SDGs, the 'greening' of the global economy, and now, also, emerging national economic strategies in the light of COVID-19.

The idea of a 'just transition' can draw on our first axiom, concerning the difference between abstract ideas and a penetrating, personal knowledge of situations, and their reality as lived; we need new research across several disciplines if the inevitable changes in our economic model are to reduce vulnerabilities and not make them worse.

A 'just transition' can draw also on our second axiom, concerning the 'ideal' that helps shape the 'real' and the imaging of peace. The challenge is to enable our 'pre-political' understanding of the good to shed light on each new set of circumstances.

In shaping our changing circumstances, we need to draw on our third axiom as well and take into account the *factors that accompany healing in a wounded social structure*. Nature and human society are not simply 'there', awaiting our choices. Complex connections are already in place and in play. Our interventions can disrupt balances and break connections. At a minimum, we must 'do no harm'. Our proper goal is to uncover the sources of benign change.

ENDS AND MEANS

Using a metaphor from archery, Aristotle states that virtue enables us to 'hit on' the mean (*aretē ... stochastikē tou mesou*), where the 'mean' is the right option among alternatives (*Nicomachean Ethics*, II.6). This virtue is, precisely, 'pre-political'; it includes an intimation of 'noble and divine things' (*Nicomachean Ethics*, X.7.1). We often forget that modern multilateral diplomacy, as conceived in response to the Holocaust and the horror of world wars, has this Aristotelian quality; it would not exist without a set of higher values to inform individual choices.

The first words of the Preamble to the UN Charter[1] are as follows:

> We the peoples of the United Nations, determined to save succeeding generations from the scourge of war.

Further high-level 'ends' are defined in the opening paragraphs of the Preamble. 'The peoples of the United Nations' are determined:

> To employ international machinery for the economic and social advancement of all peoples.

Article 1 states that among the purposes of the Charter is:

> To be a centre for harmonizing the actions of nations in the attainment of these common ends.

A similar pattern is present in the Universal Declaration of Human Rights (UDHR).[2] Article 1 states the following:

> All human beings are born free and equal in dignity and rights. They are endowed with reason and conscience and should act towards one another in a spirit of brotherhood.

Article 28 relates human dignity to life in community:

> Everyone is entitled to a social and international order in which the rights and freedoms set forth in this Declaration can be fully realized.

Articles 1 and 28 are the scaffolding on which the detailed provisions of the Universal Declaration rely; these provisions, and each subsequent decision in support of human rights, go back to questions of human origins and destiny.

THE GAP BETWEEN IDEAS AND REALITY

In the 21st century, the creative interplay of ends with means is frustrated by a widening gap between ideas and reality in at least three domains.

First, we need to re-imagine the 'Westphalian' system understood as a world order based only on the 'sovereign' decisions of nation states. The states' equal right to sovereignty does not preclude the development of new forms of socio-political organisation such as the European Union or the acceptance of 'citizenship obligations' (Haass, 2017) at the regional or global level. In the realm of national governance, our actions, to have a strong ethical foundation, need to take into account their foreseeable consequences for external stakeholders and for the common good. In this respect, political practice is behind the times. National governments, even when they grasp the need for a global dimension to policy, remain fearful of unilateral steps that may hand an advantage to other, more selfish actors. Equally, political theory is behind the times. The 'separation of powers' and other balancing devices do not, in our view, confer an absolute legitimacy on governments under today's conditions, absent a concomitant commitment to international justice and morality.

Second, in the realm of the economy, we need a clearer understanding of the relationship between profit and not-for-profit factors in our individual decision making and in shaping the marketplace at home and abroad. The COVID-19 crisis has demonstrated more clearly than ever that 'GDP' is an inadequate measure of value and as currently deployed exacerbates the problem of 'limited coverage' in the ethical sphere, which we discussed in Chapter 2.

Third, the problem of 'limited coverage' arises in an acute form as we pursue a deeper understanding of the increasingly important subject of migration. The rights of migrants are often not respected – or even well understood – within our current political economy.

In relation to these fundamental challenges – the interpretation of sovereignty under 21st-century conditions, our conceptions of economic freedom and economic productivity, and the principles that should govern migration – we are surviving from day to day, if we are honest, in a house that is badly in need of renovation. Add to this confusion our unpreparedness on environmental issues, and in 2020 the lessons of the COVID-19 pandemic, and the flimsiness of our dwelling place amounts to a crisis.

Very often, our difficulty in relating means to ends, and understanding the innate character of our decisions, hinges on a too narrow reading of the context. Even apart from the 'structural' sources of confusion, which we have just mentioned, we find it difficult to connect the situation immediately in front of us with 'what we should consistently be doing' in the light of 'the society all of us want' (Milbank and Pabst, 2016, p. 4). Below, we offer four examples of seemingly legitimate choices that become more uncomfortable the more we reflect on their implications in a wider context.

Example one

In a society in which the public health service has long waiting lists or may hardly function at all, I ensure that my own family has private health insurance. Should I ask myself whether such a choice, habitual among better-off people, slows down the development of adequate services for everyone? If the answer is 'yes', is there a way forward that enables me to protect my family while working towards the objective of universal access to healthcare?

Example two

A leading democratic society sells weapons into a country in which malnutrition or other human rights abuses are widespread. How legitimate is the argument, 'If we don't sell the arms, someone else will'?

Example three

My 'lifestyle', if I belong to the upper-middle class in a 'developed' country, can never be 'universalised' because the resources of the planet will not permit everyone in India (for example) to live as I do. Is there a moral inconsistency in my life stance? If I see an inconsistency, is it because of the principle of burden-sharing during a necessary transition, or for deeper reasons?

Example four

Historically, a very common situation is that a soldier or public official has misgivings about the context in which he works – an aggressive war, a military strategy under which planning is going forward for the use of weapons of mass destruction, a colonial administration in the midst of a popular uprising, a corrupt or dictatorial government, or simply a government wedded to dangerous policies. In the light of his own successful career under Domitian, Tacitus insists that a man can do great good under a bad prince (*De Vita Agricolae*, 42). Who would dare to say that this is not so?

THE FOCUS OF OUR POLITICAL ATTENTION

Our understanding of our responsibilities depends to a considerable degree on our vantage point. One way of looking at the world of geopolitics is to focus on the 'objective power' of certain actors (Rudd, 2020, p. 3):

> As with other historical inflection points, three factors will shape the future of the global order: changes in the relative military and economic strength of the great powers, how those changes are perceived around the world, and what strategies the great powers deploy.

This could be described as the view from the general's tent. Many of those who view the world through the flap of this tent (though not the author of the passage just quoted) are open to harsh measures. In the 'post-post-Cold War' period, a very senior British diplomat wrote as follows under the headline 'Why we still need empires':

> When dealing with old-fashioned states outside the post-modern continent of Europe, we need to revert to the rougher methods of an earlier era – force, pre-emptive attack, deception, whatever is necessary … Among ourselves we keep the law but when we are operating in the jungle, we must also use the laws of the jungle. (Cooper, 2002, n.p.)

In seeking to illuminate the moral compromises that accompany political action, Machiavelli does not deny the importance of moral values as the glue of society. However, in *The Prince*, he argues that the ruler must learn 'how not to be good' on certain well-chosen occasions. Deceit, and even cruelty, are justified by results – by their effect as measured over time – which requires very sharp judgement by the prince if his recourse to realpolitik is not to undermine the moral standards of 'ordinary people'. Max Weber appears to entertain a similar paradox in his thesis that politics is a vocation (*Beruf*) that requires a good man to leave his preferred values behind (Walzer, 1973).

The structure of these arguments is echoed in many of our contemporary discussions of torture, assassination, drone warfare, and the past and possible future use of weapons of mass destruction. We risk finding ourselves in the company of Julius Caesar who, as we saw in Chapter 2, could cut off the hands of his military opponents in the belief that it did not detract from his image or character.

The discourse around realpolitik and its supposed necessities contributes little to our understanding of everyday trade-offs and compromises as we seek to do good under a 'bad prince' or within a somewhat dysfunctional economy.

We suggest a different line of vision, more like that of the 'doomed, conscripted, un-victorious ones' (Siegfried Sassoon) than the view from the general's tent. Within our chosen line of vision, we see nation states that enjoy 'objective' power and influence but fall short in addressing public health issues, the protection of the environment, and other basic needs of citizens. Their conception of security and legitimacy is at a remove from the reality of people's lives. In the long run, their power to control events is likely to prove illusory, unless they examine the patterns of their behaviour in the light of all that they ought to know and can know, and set their course in a new way. In suggesting this, we do not ignore the view from the general's tent. On the contrary, we seek to engage with it by insisting on a broader focus of attention.

In early Indian legal theory, the term *matsyanyaya* ('fish-justice') describes a world in which the big devour the small, irrespective of the high-level rules of society (Sen, 2009, p. 20). In Roman law, there is an obligation to act in good faith, *ex bona fide*: we should not take advantage of the weak position of our partners in a transaction (Cicero, *De Officiis*, III.15, 17). When others live in squalor and have no way of sharing their talents with the community, and we have the ability to change this and do not do so, can it be said that we exercise our citizenship with an abundance of good faith? Or have we opened the doors of our world to *matsyanyaya* – to 'fish-justice'?

Our fourth axiom focuses on the shared predicament of all of us, including powerful leaders, once we acknowledge that our way of living and acting is troubling in the light of our own best insights or the concerns expressed to us by others. When society is open to positive change, 'the underlying theme in the conversation is not conflict, it is agency' (Nyabola, 2018, p. 215).

MIXED ACTIONS

Aristotle's thinking on 'mixed actions' seems to us to clarify the choices that arise once we recognise that the starting position for political deliberation is inevitably non-ideal. In particular, Aristotle clarifies the choices Machiavelli is grappling with when he advocates 'not being good', and Weber when he refers to 'the demon' that affects politics as a profession. These dilemmas, which are similar to the 'problem of dirty hands', posed by Jean-Paul Sartre in the second half of the 20th century, become a subset of the much wider problem that we act at all times within the constraints of a given situation. Humanity's future will not be secured by 'dirty hands'. It can be secured only by engaging constructively with difficult situations. We live with imperfection. We navigate the non-ideal as best we can.

Aristotle's conception of 'mixed actions' is rooted in political, as well as personal, experience.

Solon, the first great constitutional reformer at Athens, is summoned as an arbitrator when social divisions threaten the disintegration of society. The worst single aspect of the situation is the practice of enslavement for debt; Solon brings this to an end. For the rest, he does not start with a blank slate or build a settlement from scratch. His complex package of reforms to an extent reflects the existing balance of power between rich and poor as broad categories within society. No one is perfectly happy with the proposed reforms. But neither is any powerful group so discontented as to risk conflict by trying to overturn the settlement. Solon operates creatively within the de facto limits on his freedom of action. He describes this in a poem as 'finding the right fit between justice and force' (quoted in Aristotle, *Athenian Constitution*, XII.4).

For Aristotle, Pericles exemplifies the leader who can relate concrete decisions to an overall vision. In the narrative of Thucydides, Pericles sees the contradiction between the world that might be and the facts facing him, between 'pre-political values' and constrained political choices. Here is a key passage from Pericles' final speech (Thucydides, 1996, II.61.1): 'For those who have a free choice in the matter and whose fortunes are not at stake, war is the greatest of follies.'

Aristotle echoes Thucydides (*Nicomachean Ethics* X.7.6): 'No one chooses to be at war … for the sake of being at war.' Thucydides has an epigrammatic phrase to describe situations of this kind: men 'fall, without willing it, into severely limiting circumstances' (III.82:2).

Building out from the experience of leaders like Solon and Pericles, Aristotle develops the doctrine of what he terms 'mixed actions' – understandable actions that are both unfree and free because they arise within the constraints of a given situation (*miktai praxeis: Nicomachean Ethics* III.1; *Eudemian Ethics* II.8). Covering some of the same ground as Aristotle, but with less clarity, Cicero (*De Officiis* III.2) addresses the question of 'how we should make a moral discernment if that which seems morally right (*honestum*) is in conflict with what seems expedient (*utile*)'.

A 'mixed action' is by definition an uncomfortable choice: 'Actions of such a kind are voluntary, but in an ultimate sense, perhaps non-voluntary; for the reason that no one would choose any of these things for its own sake' (*Nicomachean Ethics*, III.1.6).

Aristotle considers the case of a storm at sea. If I throw my possessions overboard during a storm to save the ship from sinking, I am doing something I would never 'choose' to do, other things being equal; to that extent my action is unfree. In another perspective, throwing the goods overboard is something I decide to do; to that extent, I am acting freely. What seems justifiable, namely, to ditch the cargo, does not seem 'just' in the full sense of the word.

Aristotle presents a number of other instances of 'un-willed' action; for example, the actions of those who are drunk, or overpowered by others, or ignorant of the law. But to grasp what is meant by 'mixed action' in a political situation, it is important not to lose our way in a specialised discussion among philosophers about 'intention' and 'freedom of the will'. Agamemnon's decision, famous in Greek mythology, to kill his daughter Iphigenia to secure a fair wind for Troy, is a 'mixed action' – a political choice made under obvious duress. The issue is whether it can be justified; Iphigenia's death is not the outcome of a sudden emotional storm, nor is it the unintended secondary effect of a different decision. The question that confronts Agamemnon is whether it is right to accept a political premise and a public responsibility which 'force him' (as he thinks) to do a terrible thing. In such circumstances, should there not be an option to invoke 'the moral equivalent to our legal right not to incriminate ourselves' (Walzer, 1973, p. 165)?

PARAMETERS FOR MIXED ACTION

The challenge for political philosophy is to set parameters for 'mixed action' so that we do not end up with a Machiavellian acceptance that it is 'right to do wrong' or endorse Weber's portrait of the relentless, 'objective' leader who in choosing politics 'loses his soul' (Walzer, 1973, p. 177). We suggest five parameters for the evaluation of 'mixed action'.

Recognising the enormity of certain actions

First, some actions are ruled out by their very nature. There is a Confucian principle, 'we should not execute a blameless man even to gain an empire'. 'The things that forced Euripides' Alcmaeon to slay his mother seem absurd' (*Nicomachean Ethics*, III.1.8). We have suggested in earlier chapters that a sense of reverence or hesitation should hold us back from the 'enormity' of certain actions. Cicero twice rejects the long-term strategic argument used by the Romans to justify the destruction of Corinth ('*nollem Corinthum*': *De Officiis*, I.11; III.11). Not to tell lies or to make contradictory promises would seem to be a rule of peace-building that we should never set aside.

Proportionality

Second, it is not hard to see that proportionality is a condition of any justifiable mixed action. By way of establishing the criterion of proportion, Aristotle mentions a man who kills his opponent in anger for bumping into him in a game of blind man's bluff. Ideas of measure and proportion run through all law and every study of virtue. We can see the case for, say, avoiding sugary drinks or reducing our dependency on private motor vehicles. To ban these things altogether would be a disproportionate measure. We can promote the global public interest in the development, production, and distribution of vaccines without disregarding the interests of researchers and companies; a successful policy is likely to reflect a sense of proportion.

Motive

A third parameter, a leitmotif in the narrative of Thucydides, is the need to look carefully at our motives. Often, a supposedly reluctant decision of last resort is not, in reality, based on the impartial weighing of options in the midst of opacity. Rather, we act by force of habit, under the influence of anger or jealousy, with a view to bolstering our power for the future, or in furtherance of a self-image that blinds us to the truth of what we are doing. It would be instructive to review the best known military interventions of the 21st century from a Thucydidean angle.

Leaving space for ordinary life

Fourth, we should not allow our search for a better future to blunt our appreciation of the imperfect present. Engagement with our responsibilities is essential: to analyse every small step, or tremble all day long in fear of the consequences of what we may or may not decide to do, seems neither wise nor productive. Moments of relaxation or celebration are a part of life.

The story of the woman who poured ointment on the feet of Jesus is told differently in each of the four gospels. In St John, Judas Iscariot complains about the waste of money – according to St John, because of his corrupt management of the disciples' common fund. Jesus defends the woman's gesture as having intrinsic value, here and now, especially in the perspective of his own coming death.

Dietrich Bonhoeffer wrote the following to his fiancée in a letter from prison in March 1944 (Bonhoeffer and von Wedemeyer, 1994, p. 169):

> It's precisely because I'm already so certain of our agreement on fundamentals that we've no need to discuss the mysteries of existence all the time, but can take things as they come and continually rediscover each other in the ordinary things of life. There will be times when we're drawn to fundamentals of our own accord, but God subsists not only in fundamentals but in everyday life as well.

Overcoming the circumstances and mitigating the effects of a mixed action

Our fifth parameter is this: to the degree that we defend an action as 'mixed', as an unavoidable response to unwelcome circumstances, we are under a corresponding consequential obligation (i) to work towards overcoming the conditions that impose the necessity; and

(ii) to mitigate as much as we can the suffering caused by our action. Unless we accept such obligations, our claim to have acted under constraint is not believable.

A textbook illustration of what we mean by 'overcoming the conditions' is provided by the Nuclear Non-Proliferation Treaty (NPT).[3] Nuclear deterrence is not a strategy that we choose for its own sake. If, nevertheless, international law allows the possession of nuclear weapons by some states (an interpretation that can be disputed), that is at best a 'mixed action' on the part of the international community, something accepted under the duress of circumstances. The legitimacy of this 'mixed action' depends on a corresponding forward-looking obligation on the nuclear weapons states to work towards overall nuclear disarmament (NPT, Article VI).

To illustrate what we mean by 'mitigating the suffering' caused by a mixed action, we turn to the prison system. Deprivation of liberty is a severe punishment that can be defended as a mixed action. In practice, imprisonment is often accompanied by family breakdown, risks to health and safety, and a lifelong loss of earning capacity. According to our fifth parameter, a legitimate prison policy should seek to mitigate these 'non-necessary' consequences of imprisonment. It should also promote alternatives to imprisonment – not least because the much lower incidence of imprisonment in some social groups than in others calls into question the inherent 'necessity' of the system.

Just before his execution, Helmuth von Moltke, the leader of the Kreisau Circle,[4] wrote these words to his son (Ashdown, 2018, p. 289):

> Since National Socialism came to power, I have striven to make its consequences milder for its victims and to prepare the way for a change. In that, my conscience drove me – and in the end, that is a man's duty.

ST PAUL AND MIXED ACTION

St Paul's response to the question of chattel slavery – that most embedded and most profound of structural injustices – can be understood as a case study in 'mixed action', as applied to a wounded social structure. In a morally compromised situation, St Paul, like von Moltke, strives to make the consequences milder for victims and to prepare the way for change.

In St Paul's time, there was much discussion of slavery and the treatment of slaves among philosophers and jurists. Paradoxically, the growing jurisprudence around some aspects of slavery, including rules for manumission, had the overall effect of embedding the institution still more deeply in Roman life. Nor was it practicable to overthrow the Roman social system by direct action, as the fate of Spartacus illustrates.

In Roman history, the most significant (and humane) author on the topic of slavery is St Paul's contemporary, Seneca (Griffin, 1976; Finley, 1980; Garnsey, 1996). St Paul encountered the world of Seneca directly. The governor of Achaea who chose to overlook St Paul's missionary activity (using arguments that Pilate may initially have sought to use in the case of Jesus) was Seneca's respected older brother Junius Gallio Annaeanus (Acts 18). Seneca was still a key advisor to Nero when St Paul 'appealed to Caesar' (though within five or six years, both Gallio and Seneca, like St Paul, had fallen victim to the Emperor Nero's repressions).

Both Seneca and St Paul regard slavery as an institution 'against nature'. St Paul improves on the 'progressive' consensus of his time in three main ways.

Prescinding from the 'back story'

There was a well-known Stoic paradox, 'Every good man is free, every bad man is a slave'. On this view, both masters and slaves should accept the workings of 'chance', or 'fortune', or 'fate', and concentrate on self-development.

Jesus has no interest in 'fortune', 'fate', or any back story to explain disability:

> Rabbi, who sinned, this man or his parents, for him to have been born blind?
> Neither he nor his parents sinned. He was born blind so that the works of God might be displayed in him. As long as the day lasts, I must carry out the work of the one who sent me.
>
> (John 9:1–5; cf. Luke 13:4–5 on those killed by the collapse of a tower)

Because the teaching of Jesus is forward-looking in this way, St Paul has the room he needs to treat the situation of master and slave as 'given' only in a contingent sense. There is no 'back story' that entitles a slave-owner to act as he sees fit within the limits of his role.

The opening passage of Aristotle's *Politics* differentiates among human beings in terms of three basic distinctions: man/woman, master/slave, and Greek/barbarian. St Paul implicitly challenges Aristotle. In Galatians (3:27–28), he rejects, in the name of Christ, the dichotomies male and female, master and slave, Jew and Greek. In Colossians (3:11), St Paul adds that there is no 'barbarian, Scythian, slave'. Similar arguments are presented in the First Letter to the Corinthians (12:13) and (minus the listing of categories) in other letters.

Speaking directly to slaves

Seneca writes as one 'humane' slave-owner to another, especially in a famous letter to his friend Lucilius (Seneca, 1917, *Epistula* XLVII, pp. 301 –313). St Paul's communications on slavery are intended to be heard by both slave and master. The First Letter to the Corinthians includes the following messages (7:20–24):

> If you can gain your freedom, take the opportunity.
>
> (Verse 21)
>
> Do not become the slaves of men.
>
> (Verse 23)

This whole passage is governed by the qualification, 'this is from me and not from the Lord' (7:12). St Paul offers prudential advice.

Taking a forward-looking view

The Passover commemorates a release from slavery (Ochs, 2020). The language of redemption in the New Testament suggests the payment made to a slave-holder to secure the freeing of a slave (*lytron*: Hart, 2017, p. 556). John the Baptist, Jesus, and their disciples do not themselves own slaves. The episode in which Jesus washes the feet of the disciples is emblematic in this respect (John 13:3–18). St Paul's Letter to Philemon is the only part of the New Testament devoted entirely to a contemporary issue in Roman law. It is an open communication that is clearly intended to have 'demonstration value'.

The Letter does not acknowledge an obligation to send the slave Onesimus back to his master; on the contrary, St Paul openly contemplates not sending him back (verses 13–14). Legally and politically, St Paul is treading on dangerous ground. Is he encouraging slaves to run away?

St Paul's solution to this 'micro' situation of considerable delicacy goes further than an appeal to the sophistication and virtue of the slave-owner. Paul seeks an assurance from Philemon that Onesimus, if he returns, will no longer be treated in the usual way, as a slave would be liable to be treated under Roman law and custom: 'not as a slave any more, but something much better than a slave, a dear brother' (verse 16).

As mentioned in Chapter 4, St Paul describes himself as the *koinōnos* of both Philemon and Onesimus (verse 17); he is 'in communion with' both. This, we have suggested, takes the Greek political concept of a 'shared life' in a new direction. The 'shared life' of master and slave in one well-advertised case will have consequences at the 'macro' level for anyone who pauses to reflect – consequences for sexual access to slaves (which was standard), branding on the face (which was common), breaking up families, the forms of punishment reserved for slaves, having slaves kill one another for entertainment in the arena, the vicious abuses of the slave trade, and ultimately for the institution of slavery itself. Seneca had already seen clearly that treating slaves humanely, as 'fellow members of a household' (*familiares*), could have implications for the institution of slavery: 'Some may maintain that I am offering liberty to slaves in general, and toppling masters from their high estate, because I said, "they should respect their master instead of fearing him"' (Seneca, 1917, p. 311, translation slightly adapted).

St Paul's strategy is a classic Aristotelian mixed action, applied to a wounded social structure. He works for transformation 'from within' by persuading the slave-owner to accept a forward-looking obligation that alters, in practice, the workings of the institution and thereby opens, implicitly, a pathway to reform.

MIXED ACTION IN THE 21ST CENTURY

Aristotle experiments with broad applications of the concept of mixed action. As we have seen, war is a mixed action that can only be considered if there is a prospect of building peace. At times, the holding of slaves and even a money-based economy are seen through a similar lens:

If every tool could perform its own work when ordered ... like the tripods of Hephaestus [used by the gods] ... masters would have no need of slaves.

(Politics, I.2)

The life of money-making is one undertaken under compulsion ... for it is useful for the sake of something else.

(Nicomachean Ethics I.5)

In the perspective of our planetary future, a way of life bound up with current patterns of consumption can be read as a 'mixed action' – acceptable, perhaps, because of the constraints of our situation, and because ordinary life should continue, but only to the degree that we accept a corresponding forward-looking obligation to work 'from within' to change what can be changed in the battle against carbon emissions, environmental degradation, and the loss of biodiversity.

The American economist and political thinker E. Glen Weyl (2019, p. 24) proposes a political methodology that sounds very much like mixed action:

To the maximum extent possible, erosion [of concentrations of power] should occur in ways that harness and beat existing power structures at their own game, rather than through extra-system means that could precipitate violence.

Pope Francis formulates the following principle:

Conscience ... can also recognize with sincerity and honesty what for now is the most generous response which can be given to God, and come to see with a certain moral security that it is what God himself is asking amid the concrete complexity of one's limits, while not yet fully the objective ideal.

(Amoris Laetitia, 303, 2016)

LATENT POTENTIAL

In interpreting our life-stance as a 'mixed action', we have, as it were, an alibi and a working explanation – all the more so, if we invoke the distinction between what is 'possible' here and now and 'the latent potential' that can be enabled by our actions.

The Islamic thinker Avicenna develops the powerfully enabling idea that the potential evolution of any political situation is always more far-reaching than what is immediately 'possible'. To use a modern example, the 'latent potential' to build aeroplanes was, in some sense, always there. But aeroplanes only became 'possible' as a result of several intervening scientific and experimental break-throughs. The 'potential' to abolish slavery was present, or latent, in the antebellum South. How and when abolition became politically 'possible' is a matter for debate.

Ernst Bloch builds on Avicenna's observations to challenge the Aristotelian understanding of 'form' and 'potentiality' and to assert the possibility of radically new developments in which human agency can play its part (Bloch, 1952, 2019): 'Truth [is] the reflection of reality and the power to exert an influence upon reality' (quoted in Lash, 1981, p. 84).

Rabbi Jonathan Sacks (2009, pp. 231–252), from a very different perspective, explores the 'nature and significance of the future tense'. The creativity and care of God, as revealed to Moses, means that the future is open, unknowable, and full of hope. The core of Rabbi Sacks's argument is that Exodus 3:14, *Ehyeh asher ehyeh*, is rightly translated 'I will be what I choose to be'.

The 'evolutionary potential' of international cooperation today is difficult to gauge. What we can say with certainty is that the 'possi-ble' steps we take here and now, even steps of a procedural character, can liberate a latent evolutionary 'potential'; a better future as yet unseen can become visible for the first time.

An example of a 'possible' step that might release 'evolutionary potential' would be the systematic development of regional and inter-regional cooperation as an essential element of a decentralis-ing multilateral order. We argue in this book that a cross-disciplinary focus on religion and human values enabled by the convening power of international organisations would represent a further seminal change, especially if accompanied by new political mechanisms to ensure 'accessibility', as we will discuss in Chapter 6. The Epilogue suggests that no region is better placed than Europe to promote these liberating intermediate steps.

In diplomacy, a clearer awareness that all governments work within non-ideal situations full of hidden potential should make it much easier to engage with others as equals, explore compromises, and decide on next steps. 'Mixed action' and 'latent potentiality' together create a conceptual space in which we can allow ourselves more time, making space for a gradual transition, but in which the exponents of non-moral *raisons d'état* will have less room to operate.

OUR FIFTH AXIOM: SCANNING FOR UNSEEN JUSTICE

A SYMBIOSIS OF VALUES AND INTERESTS?

The unexamined assumption underlying the foreign policy of many governments is that we are in a 'good place', morally speaking; that our political positioning is on the side of history; that our values and our economic interests largely converge; and (at least in many cases) that we deserve credit for offering development or humanitarian assistance to the less fortunate. To protect our interests, we invest heavily in means of enforcement (we are 'global security providers'). At the same time, we use persuasion to advance our values when persuasion works (we understand 'soft power').

Under this paradigm, the conflict that we see between values and interests occurs on a narrow front: we cooperate, as a matter of self-interest, with states that do not 'share our values'.

The UN Security Council, or in some circumstances a broad range of states acting together, might impose an arms embargo or some other measure with a view to containing a threat to international security; in that sense, situations arise in which we privilege our values over those of others. However, in the exercise of what is sometimes termed 'economic statecraft', there is a risk that the imagined symbiosis of our values and our economic interests will nurture a mindset marked by complacency. We may find it hard to look in the mirror wondering whether we too fail, whether we too end up on the wrong side of the ledger, whether we too need forgiveness for the past, whether we too are accountable to values that we find it hard to realise in practice. We may divide the world into friends and adversaries and then embrace a contradiction: seeking the good will of other governments on important issues for us, while at the same time adopting measures that, in their eyes, are deliberately harming their people. Too much of a 'double-track' approach and we lapse into a harsh, self-referential, mechanical understanding of human relationships.

The idea that our own values and interests converge and that our neighbour's values are more like a smokescreen or a matter of chance can amount, in the end, to withdrawing from dialogue and denying shared moral responsibility. Our fifth axiom is that *discernment in the midst of opacity in accordance with a common standard should become a core value in the conduct of international relations.*

THE DIPLOMACY OF THE TWO STANDARDS

In political and diplomatic situations, the formulation of alternatives is an important stage in the process of discernment. Situations are dynamic, and the future is by definition uncertain. If we are not to lapse into confusion and cross-purposes, it is useful at certain moments to enter imaginatively into the space we share with others and formulate a choice. In private life, we see this clearly: to marry or not to marry; to migrate or to stay. In 2020, confronting the risks posed by the coronavirus, public health authorities have seen that for decision-making purposes, it is helpful for the multitude of conceivable policy responses to coalesce around broad alternatives.

An important skill is to frame these key choices in such a way as to see what is mainly at stake from an ethical perspective. Very often, the way forward reflects either of two 'standards':

- on the one hand, a 'self-interested' standard that promises tangible benefits in the short term, though it may ignore some moral claims
- on the other hand, a standard more trusting of others, more in accordance with a traditional understanding of honourable conduct, more geared to the long term, more attuned to common benefits that are not easily measured

Framing our decisions as a series of choices between two standards is, in itself, an exercise of the historical imagination. In each instance, the first alternative, the 'standard of self-interest', may tempt us. An intimation of better values may cause us to hesitate.

APPLYING THE STANDARD OF JUSTICE 'ADDS UP'

Choices made in accordance with the second, more trusting standard are broadly in harmony, across time and space, with other choices made in accordance with the same standard, including other people's choices. The second standard – let us call it the 'standard of justice' – enables us to link one situation to another and to give the future a certain shape or character, even before the detailed picture becomes clear.

We argued in Chapter 4 that when Jesus states that 'the weightier part of the law is discernment, mercy, and faith', the gift of discernment (*krisis*) invites us to analyse the social space that we share with others in terms of policy alternatives.

Gandhian satyagraha, or 'action in the truth', is a specific form of discernment in the midst of opacity in accordance with a common standard. Gandhi applied analogous non-violent strategies in a number of different situations: to achieve the Indian Relief Act in Natal, to oppose unjust rents in the Champaran Movement in Bihar, in a similar campaign in Gujarat, and in the Salt Satyagraha of 1930. To understand the logic of any one of these campaigns leads to a ready understanding of all the others. All have demonstrative value in a much bigger picture. In each case, it is in the long-term interests even of Gandhi's opponents to recognise the merits of his position.

The emerging policy of the EU on climate change, the 'European Green Deal', implies, in its intellectual structure, most of what we are trying to say here about 'mixed action' and the 'standard of justice'. As European citizens, 'we are proud of where we are' (von der Leyen, 2019) – yet 'where we are' is not where we need to be. Therefore, the EU is committed to an ambitious, equitable agenda of transformation. A 'just transition for all', to borrow again the language of President von der Leyen, depends on numerous individual decisions linked together by a common criterion of evaluation. This common criterion cannot be the standard of self-interest as described above. It will resemble much more the 'standard of justice'.

Scanning for the 'unseen justice' in each particular situation can help mend the principal fault line in today's global culture. That is, we can help resolve the tension between a conception of the human person as an independent, choice-making individual on the one hand, and, on the other hand, a conception of the human person that includes relationships with others, with the common good of society, and, in some sense, with the planet itself. It is overwhelmingly in our long-term interest to trust the 'standard of justice' and thereby find a sustainable point of convergence between our separate, individual interests and the overall common interest.

THE COMMON CRITERION OF HOPE

The orientation and methodology that we promote through our six axioms aim to achieve a balance between the interweaving of different countries' interests, an interweaving which is tangible and ongoing, and the interaction of consciences, which seems to take place only at the margins of international politics. In combination, our guiding ideas imply a particular understanding of hope. Above all, our fifth axiom reflects a shared or common hope by urging us to choose justice over self-interest. Our disparate wagers on the future are similar in character, like buds on one stem.

Hope requires courage – upright action for the sake of the future. Hope is rational – an escapist fantasy does not qualify as hope in action. In his inaugural lecture as Professor of Poetry at Oxford, Seamus Heaney quotes Vaclav Havel on hope (Heaney, 1995, pp. 4–5):

> a state of mind, not a state of the world ... an orientation of the spirit, of the heart; it transcends the world that is immediately experienced, and is anchored somewhere beyond its horizons ... It is not the conviction that something will turn out well, but the certainty that something makes sense, regardless of how it turns out.

Traditional religious thinkers analyse hope as the mean between presumption and despair. In Pope Benedict's encyclical on hope, '*Spe Salvi*', the focus has switched from our inner equilibrium to realities outside ourselves – to 'the impossibility that the injustice of history should be the final word'.

That 'something makes sense, regardless of how it turns out', and 'the impossibility that the injustice of history should be the final word', are dynamic assertions; they imply a readiness to act, even in the face of steep odds. Hope, if restored to its full meaning in our culture, can inspire and bring together all those who face the future, determined to be 'part of the solution' – all those willing to serve under the banner of justice to bring consolation and healing to an ailing society.

In what follows, we provide a brief 'sketch' of hope, drawing on mutually reinforcing religious, literary, and philosophical sources; the 'literacy' or 'life-stance' reflected in our axioms arises naturally from 'experiments with truth' that do not depend on a specific religious understanding of the world. Nevertheless, for the believer, hope in God completes and also transforms our picture of reality.

A story beyond this world helps us make sense of what is happening here and now. In the words of the Mahabharata: 'like a temple bell calling him out of sorrow and futility, Krishna's words rang in the morning' (Menon, 2004, p. 162).

HOPE CAN BE PERCEIVED AS SOMETHING 'GIVEN'

In his *Theogony*, one of the first works of Western literature, Hesiod claims a relationship with a source of truth that is both personal and of divine origin – namely the Muses encountered in the mists of Mount Helicon. Hesiod grapples with the inspiration given to him by the Muses and goes on to produce a public poetry directed towards the world of politics and society. Without the initial encounter, which is entirely 'given', Hesiod would be just another 'hungry shepherd'.

Seamus Heaney's images of the 'tidal wave' and 'cloudburst' imply the 'given-ness' of historical change. For Heaney, personal commitment and integrity are essential virtues in politics, as in writing poetry. In the end, greatness, whether in politics or poetry, is 'given', at least in part.

Below, we use the mission of Virgil's Aeneas to illustrate the communal dimension of hope. Aeneas depends at several key moments on a vision, a dream, a divine messenger. Aeneas is never self-sufficient. What he senses to be the requirements of his situation needs affirmation.

HOPE PROVIDES A COMMON CRITERION OF MEASUREMENT

Congresswoman Alexandria Ocasio-Cortez (2018) wrote an article in *America* magazine on criminal justice reform, beginning with a personal story flowing from the statement, 'I believe in the forgiveness of sins'. In the light of this premise, Ocasio-Cortez takes up a number of different issues in the realm of criminal justice. Then she turns again to the level of principle at which criminal justice reform converges with other projects: 'By nature, a society that forgives and rehabilitates its people is a society that forgives and transforms itself.'

To argue that a new look at imprisonment can support wider social objectives is not just about shaping coalitions. That can happen, certainly. But the point is deeper and goes to the heart of our vision in this book. As we argue above in relation to Gandhian satyagraha, something that they have in common links all situations in which justice and hope are at stake.

HOPE AS 'GOING AGAINST THE CURRENT'

Greek philosophers associate the virtues of hope and courage. In political decision making, as we have argued above, we are drawn towards one or other of two standards: the self-interested or the more generous option. The second option is the option of hope. Compared to the first option, it often requires exceptional courage, especially the moral courage of embarking on a journey towards an unknown destination, or a journey that will only be completed by others after our time. 'Radical hope anticipates a good for which those who have the hope as yet lack the appropriate concepts with which to understand it' (Jonathan Lear, quoted in Mittleman, 2009, p. 158). Seret arbores, qui alteri saeculo prosint ('he plants trees for the benefit of another age') (Statius, quoted by Cicero, Tusculan Disputations, XIV).

HOPE ACCORDS WITH REASON

In the Hebrew prophets, genuine hope comes with an ethical dimension and a certain kind of realism. Jeremiah opposes the wishful thinking, false optimism, and empty hope of his rival Hananiah.

A crucial aspect of the prophetic tradition is that hope can go against the current of events and yet remain reasonable. Jeremiah purchases land just as the kingdom of Judah is being overrun by the Babylonians (Jeremiah 32:13):

> In their presence, I gave Baruch these instructions: 'Take these deeds, the sealed deed of purchase and its open copy, and put them in an earthenware pot, so that they may be preserved for a long time.' For Yahweh Sabaoth, the God of Israel, says this, 'People will buy fields and vineyards in this land again.'

In the Greek tradition, the classic case of a slim or forlorn hope, that at the same time is reasonable and even noble, is the Athenians' decision to abandon Athens to the Persians and stake the future of their democracy on the sea battle at Salamis. The object of our love or hope is never a matter of indifference. It is when divorced from good intentions and good judgement that hope becomes morally dangerous.

HOPE CAN BECOME A STABLE DISPOSITION

Our fifth observation about hope is that it is better understood as a stable disposition than as an attitude or an emotion. A number of insights follow once we regard hope as a 'stable disposition'. For one thing, hope can take root as a result of repeated choices. Our understanding of hope, like our understanding of love within a relationship, can develop gradually. If hope is a disposition, it can survive our momentary lapses – as in the soliloquies of Hamlet, or when the marshal in *High Noon* retreats for a few moments to a dark stable. The disposition of hope can also be nurtured or revived by the sympathetic interest of others.

Hope as a 'stable disposition' begins to have an 'objective' quality; it a well-spring of action and even an intellectual resource – a radar through which to probe the darkness.

HOPE IS SHARED

In the journey of Aeneas from Troy to Latium, Virgil (2005)[5] offers us a case study in the communal dimension of hope.

Following the storm in Book I, Aeneas, for the sake of his men, 'puts on a brave face', 'simulates hope' (*spem vultu simulat; Aeneid* I.209). A large part of Aeneas's loyalty to the given task, his *pietas*, is the ability to continue to act 'as if' for the sake of others.

In Dido's Carthage, Aeneas notices images of the Trojan War painted on a wall (*Aeneid* I.461): *Sunt lacrimae rerum* ('there are tears in history'). But others' recognition of Trojan suffering, their 'com-passion' in the literal sense, touches Aeneas decisively. As a result of this communication through art, Aeneas begins to 'hope for salvation' (*sperare salutem*) (*Aeneid* I.451).

Almost the only words spoken by Aeneas to his son are these:

> disce, puer, virtutem ex me verumque laborem,
> fortunam ex aliis.
>
> (XII.435–436)

> (From me, boy, learn courage and what work really means;
> good fortune, you must learn from others).

Aeneas knows that he will not live long to enjoy his marriage to Lavinia or to benefit from the arrangement he makes in Latium to settle his Trojan survivors. It is true that out of Aeneas's long struggle, over stages lasting hundreds of years, Rome and the Roman Empire will come to birth; the cause of Rome provides a kind of impersonal 'eschatology' in the Aeneid. But at the end of Book VI, having glimpsed the whole of reality and a glorious Roman future, Aeneas leaves the underworld by the 'ivory gate', the route by which *falsa insomnia*, delusive dreams, escape to the upper world (VI.896).

Aeneas does not have a perfect character; he is dependent on divine assistance. He is not blessed with happiness; nor does Roman destiny provide a secure basis for personal hope. Nevertheless, the journey from Troy to Italy is a forward-looking, communal endeavour that bears fruit; *sperare salutem*, the 'hope of salvation', becomes a source of meaning.

A particular feature of Aeneas's 'stable disposition' is that it is directed towards a goal that is never quite clear. A city named after himself ('Aeneadae' in Thrace) is not the right answer, nor is the 'little Troy' established by Helenus on the Greek coast. Aeneas must continue onwards towards the *arva Ausonia*, the 'Ausonian fields', *semper cedentia retro*, 'ever-receding before him' (III.496).

Abraham is prepared to live in a tent for the sake of a city he will never see. Moses wanders in the desert and dies before reaching the Promised Land. Abraham and Moses, like Aeneas, are working for others and for an unseen future. But much more than Aeneas, Abraham and Moses have a clear vocation: they are called by a God in whom they can trust absolutely and who exercises His power on humanity's behalf. 'I am with you always to the close of the age', promises the risen Jesus (Matthew 28:20).

From the perspective of religious hope, as contrasted with the dogged piety of Aeneas, life can be a joyful task that brings us closer to others. To continue working for a more just arrangement of human affairs makes complete sense, even when we fail; the meaning or pattern in events shines out in the perspective of eternity.

The Bhagavad Gita insists on the quality of an action, irrespective of results. The 'given-ness' of the fruits of action, and the confidence that somehow, somewhere the seed sown by upright action in a former generation will come to a ripening, is central to the religious perspective on human experience.

For many believers, there is something of God's grace, of mystery, even in our basic ability to live, know, and communicate. To explore the full resonance of a word like 'love' or 'hope', or, of course, to love another person, or hope in them, takes us to places where nothing is fully measurable, and nothing can be forced. The consolation of music or art involves a leap from shape to significance.

The 21st century needs upright and committed action at all levels of society for the sake of our future life in common. Religious hope adds light and energy to the efforts of very many people:

> Do not fear, for I have redeemed you; I have called you by name, you are mine. When you pass through the sea, I will be with you; and through the rivers, they shall not overwhelm you; when you walk through fire you shall not be burned, and the flame shall not consume you.
>
> (Isaiah 43:1–2)

The religious hope of some subtracts nothing from those others who reach out towards the future without seeking a religious explanation – or who may even remain wary, in the light of history, of crystallising human values in any broad philosophy. In this volume, we do not argue for theocracy in any form; we argue merely that to try to exclude God and religion from the conversation about our global future is to aim deliberately low.

The taking of power to ourselves, in one form or another, is at the root of the suffering of hundreds of millions of people, and poses a grave risk for humanity and for the planet. A culture of encounter founded on the humility that it takes to listen to one another, and of discernment founded on an antecedent openness to the truth of situations, can lead us to act together in hope as if a merciful God exists. This disposition – adopted for the sake of others as well as for ourselves – can become, in the French phrase, *le provisoire qui dure* ('the provisional that lasts'); an initial hypothesis can become the habit of hope. Here lies a viable 21st-century alternative to the 'law of the strongest' in international relations.

NOTES

1 The UN Charter (including the Preamble) can be found at www.un.org> charter-united-nations.
2 The UDHR can be viewed at www.un.org>universal-declaration-human-rights.
3 The NPT can be viewed at https://www.un.org/disarmament/wmd/nuclear/npt/.

4   The Kreisau Circle (*Der Kreisauer Kreis*) became one of the most significant of the overlapping groups that opposed the Hitler regime. It is named
after the von Moltke estate in Silesia where it met from 1940 to 1944.
Its members included men and women, socialists and devout Catholics or
Protestants. The Kreisau Circle studied the conditions that permitted the
rise of National Socialism and explored new and creative approaches to
economics, politics, and European cooperation, for implementation once
Hitler was overthrown. Most of the Circle's members were discovered
by the Gestapo and executed. Their ideas and their witness continue to
inspire the ecumenical movement and are one of the foundations of today's
European Union (Leustean, 2014).

5   Virgil. (2005). *Aeneid*, translated by Stanley Lombardo. Indianapolis: Hackett
Publishing Company.

REFERENCES

Aristotle. (1932). *Politics*, translated by H. Rackham. Loeb Classical Library.
Cambridge: Harvard University Press.

Aristotle. (1935). *The Athenian Constitution, The Eudemian Ethics, On Virtues and
Vices*, translated by H. Rackham. Loeb Classical Library. Cambridge: Harvard
University Press.

Aristotle. (1972 [1925]). *Nicomachean Ethics*, translated with an introduction by
Sir David Ross. London: Oxford University Press.

Ashdown, P. and Young, S. (2018). *Nein! Standing Up to Hitler 1935–1944*. London:
William Collins.

Bloch, E. (2019). *Avicenna and the Aristotelian Left*, translated by L. Goldman and
P. Thompson. New York: Columbia Press (original German version, 1952).

Bonhoeffer, D. and von Wedemeyer, M. (1994). *Love Letters from Cell 92*. London:
Harper Collins.

Chan, J. (2014). *Confucian Perfectionism: A Political Philosophy for Modern Times*.
Princeton and Oxford: Princeton University Press.

Cicero. (1913). *De Officiis*, translated by W. Miller. Loeb Classical Library.
Cambridge: Harvard University Press.

Cicero. (1927). *Tusculan Disputations*, translated by J.E. King. Loeb Classical
Library. Cambridge: Harvard University Press.

Cooper, R. (2002). 'Why We Still Need Empires,' *Observer*, 7 April.

Finley, M. (1980). *Ancient Slavery and Modern Ideology*. London: Chatto and
Windus.

Garnsey, P. (1996). *Ideas of Slavery from Aristotle to Augustine*. Cambridge:
Cambridge University Press.

Griffin, M. (1976). *Seneca: A Philosopher in Politics*. Oxford: Oxford University Press.

Haass, R. (2017). *A World in Disarray: American Foreign Policy and the Crisis of the Old Order*. New York: Penguin Press.

Hart, D.B. (2017). *The New Testament*. New Haven and London: Yale University Press.

Heaney, S. (1995). *The Redress of Poetry*. London: Faber and Faber.

Lash, N. (1981). *A Matter of Hope: A Theologian's Reflections on the Thought of Karl Marx*. London: Darton, Longman, and Todd.

Leustean, L.N. (2014). *The Ecumenical Movement and the Making of the European Community*. Oxford: Oxford University Press.

Machiavelli. (1961). *The Prince*, translated with an introduction by George Bull. London: Penguin Books.

Menon, R. (2004). *The Mahabharata: A Modern Rendering*, Vol 2. New Delhi: Rupa & Co.

Milbank, J. and Pabst, A. (2016). *The Politics of Virtue: Post-Liberalism and the Human Future*. London: Rowman & Littlefield International.

Mittleman, A. (2009). *Hope in a Democratic Age: Philosophy, Religion, and Political Theory*. Oxford: Oxford University Press.

Nyabola, N. (2018). *Digital Democracy, Analogue Politics: How the Internet Era Is Transforming Kenya (African Arguments)*. London: Zed Books.

Ocasio-Cortez, A. (2018). 'I Believe in the Forgiveness of Sins,' *America*, 27 June 2018.

Ochs, V. (2020). *The Passover Haggadah: A Biography*. Princeton and Oxford: Princeton University Press.

Rudd, K. (2020). 'The Coming Post-COVID Anarchy: The Pandemic Bodes Ill for Both American and Chinese Power – and for the Global Order,' *Foreign Affairs*, May/June.

Sacks, J. (2009). *Future Tense: A Vision for Jews and Judaism in the Global Culture*. London. Hodder & Stoughton.

Sen, A. (2010). *The Idea of Justice*. London: Penguin Books.

Seneca. (1917). *Epistulae Morales: Letters I–LXV*, with an English translation by R.M. Gummere. Loeb Classical Library. Cambridge: Harvard University Press.

Tacitus. (1967). *De Vita Agricolae*, edited by R.M. Ogilvie and I. Richmond. Oxford: Clarendon Press.

Thucydides. (1996). *The Landmark Thucydides: A Comprehensive Guide to the Peloponnesian War* (revised edition of the Richard Crawley translation), edited by R.B. Strassler. New York: Free Press.

Virgil. (1969). *Vergili Opera*, edited by R.A.B. Mynors. Oxford: Clarendon Press.

Virgil. (2005). *Aeneid*, translated by S. Lombardo. Indianapolis: Hackett Publishing Company.

Von der Leyen, U. (2019). *A Union that Strives for More: My Agenda for Europe. Political Guidelines for the Next European Commission 2019–2024*. Brussels: European Commission.

Walzer, M. (1973). 'The Problem of Dirty Hands,' *Philosophy & Public Affairs*, 2(2), 160–180.

Weyl, E.G. (2019). 'The Political Philosophy of RadicalxChange.' www.radicalxchange.org/blog/posts/2019-12-30

6

THE DEVELOPMENT OF NEW FRAMEWORKS OF ENGAGEMENT

THE IMPORTANCE OF METHODOLOGY

Our sixth axiom is that *a changing diplomatic culture requires the development of new frameworks of engagement.* Our goal in this chapter is to clarify some of the conditions under which a values-led dialogue inclusive of religious traditions, and reflecting the decency of ordinary people, can help make multilateralism fit for purpose.

Democratic societies have been founded on two ideas that are in tension with one another. On the one hand, there are shared values – at the minimum, a shared story, a shared understanding of the dangers to be avoided, and shared institutions. On the other hand, nothing is finally fixed. Once the people have taken a major decision, they can always use the same rules to change direction. We create a welfare state; alternatively, we reject 'big government'. Britain can join the EU or leave it again. A state can amend its constitution. The tension between stability and freedom can work well, but only in a context of mutual respect, awareness of shared interests, and serious deliberation about the future.

Our political journey has become more difficult in the 21st century, for several reasons. There is a mismatch between the 'electoral cycle' and the scale of the problems to be addressed, which require long-term strategies. Public debate is often fragmented. 'Everyone has a voice', thanks to social media; but who is listening?

Democratic deliberation about the future is disconnected from reality when, as often happens, we are unable to give due weight to the global dimension of major problems. The global economy is shaped by a complex web of relationships in which the links between cause and effect, between voter preference and real-world outcome, are often impossible to grasp.

Many of the tensions that are a feature of liberal democracy are also relevant in societies based on different political premises. Mutual respect, awareness of shared interests, and serious deliberation about the future are as important for China as for the US.

Some societies are beginning to 'image' the future, not in the sense of making exact predictions, but in the poet Shelley's (2003, p. 677) sense of 'foreknowing the spirit of events'. The 'Global Strategy'[1] of the EU, adopted in 2016, looks forward to 'a rules-based global order with multilateralism as its key principle and the United Nations at its core'. Reviewing the global strategy in 2019, the EU commits itself to upholding international norms; extending multilateralism to new areas; and making multilateral organisations fit for purpose. Post-pandemic – when the worst of the COVID-19 crisis has passed – it is probable that many people will be open to an ambitious imaging of the future.

The stated priorities of Commission President Ursula von der Leyen include a leadership role for the EU in such areas as climate change, the implementation of the SDGs, the reform of the WTO, and defining standards for data protection and the new generation of technologies (von der Leyen, 2019). During the COVID-19 crisis, the Commission is also focusing on public health issues and economic and budgetary strategy.

> The horrors of world war and the evils of fascism and communism are not in the memories of today's young people. For them, Europe needs a new *raison d'être*. I believe dealing with challenges that can be overcome only through collective, multilateral action must be that *raison d'être*, with climate action first.
>
> (Varadkar, 2020)

These are the words of the then Irish Taoiseach, Leo Varadkar, in early 2020. Can the EU reach young people, and people who take little interest in politics, with a message that institutions such as the Commission and the European Central Bank are relevant to the daily experience of citizens and reflect the profound vision of reconciliation, solidarity, and peace that lies behind the EU's founding treaties?

In this book, we argue that 'a rules-based global order with multilateralism as its key principle' and 'a new *raison d'être* for Europe' will depend in part on a cultural transition, a rekindling of dormant aspects of our political and social imagination. New 'places and practices of hope' (Ward, 2020) are a strand to be woven into a comprehensive pattern of change.

As we have argued in earlier chapters, what is not achievable today or tomorrow may become possible in the future. Action even on a limited scale, away from what appears to be the main stage of history, can be the catalyst. A helpful step towards imaging an age of sharing at the global level is to develop the right orientation and methodology for the conduct of diplomacy.

The poet Lorca (1960, p. 382) paints a picture of a sombre, striving 'horseman of the plains' galloping towards distant Cordova. The horseman 'knows the roads'; he is well equipped; but death is watching him from afar. Does Lorca's poem describe our global situation? What is certain is that unless we know the roads and prepare our maps and compasses, we can never even attempt that brave journey across the plains. If issues are not discussed with reference to context and purpose, they will not be solved effectively. Frameworks of engagement need to be created where we can think 30 years ahead, in a global perspective, in the light of what is best in human nature. Unless we make good methodological decisions, the destination of a life worthy of our humanity will remain forever on the distant horizon – *lejana y sola*, like Cordova in the poem.

THE TIMELINE OF HISTORY

Before turning to the nuts and bolts of future consultations or negotiations, we will elaborate further on the civilisational issues at stake with the help of Osip Mandelstam and Seamus Heaney, two poets who have already been summoned as witnesses in this book.

The external background to the poems of Osip Mandelstam's maturity is the overwhelming change for the worse brought about by war and revolution. An untitled poem of 1918 (Mandelstam, 2008, pp. 202–203) refers to the city of St Petersburg/Petrograd as 'Petropolis'. In calling the much-loved city 'Petropolis', as Pushkin had also done, Mandelstam evokes the world of the Greek *polis* and links the fate of the city to the course of civilisation itself.

Throughout the poem, Mandelstam addresses a distant star as the 'brother' of Petropolis. The star is a 'wandering fire' or 'giant ship' at a terrible height. The point about the 'terrible height' is that the star and what it may stand for are too far away to make a difference. The star is 'transparent', *prozrachnaya*, implying ghostliness, a loss of purchase on reality. Since the star seems not to be efficacious, Mandelstam almost begins to doubt its identity. Nevertheless, he ends the poem praying to the star on behalf of the suffering city. There is no exit from the situation other than to appeal to the very source of truth whose significance is called into question in the poem.

If we are to imagine the history of a civilisation as following a timeline, Mandelstam sees himself as living at a late stage, under a drifting or a dying star; the old values are fading.

A star that loses purchase on reality can serve as an image, in certain ways, for the drift in the direction of 'symbolic politics' in many of our democracies and for the wider drift towards international disorder. Seamus Heaney tells us in his Nobel Lecture (Heaney, 1995, p. 14) that his understanding of the place of poetry in society was shaped largely by Mandelstam's example. For Heaney, our historical context at the beginning of the 21st century is a tired 'aftermath', following colonialism and our 20th-century world wars: 'the documents of civilization have been written in blood and tears … the inclination is not only not to credit human nature with much constructive potential but not to credit anything too positive in the work of art' (Heaney, 1995, p. 19).

Heaney does not remain in an abject posture. His vision of hope for Ireland is expressed in several individual poems, in the Nobel Lecture, and perhaps above all in the image of 'the tidal wave of justice' in his famous adaptation of a play of Sophocles (Heaney, 1990, p. 77).

Broadly speaking, Heaney's career is the literary counterpart of the process that led to the Good Friday (Belfast) Agreement in 1998.

For Mandelstam or Heaney, that we are humbled by our history does not rule out new 'political possibilities'. Mandelstam saw his life's work as expressing 'nostalgia for a world culture'. The core of Heaney's Nobel Lecture is that we should 'credit the possibility of a world where respect for the validity of every tradition will issue in the creation and maintenance of a salubrious political space' (Heaney, 1995, p. 23). In imagining the timeline of history in a new way, we do not rule out Heaney's 'tidal wave of justice' – or as he puts it elsewhere, the 'cloudburst' that transforms everything (Heaney, 1987, p. 47). But barring the political equivalent of a tsunami, a positive change in the pattern of our culture is likely to occur gradually. Therefore, to credit the potential for a 'more salubrious political space' at the global level is to think in terms of a strategy devised for one or two generations.

LIFE LIES IN THE PROCESSES

In the Introduction, we argued that an effective dialogue about the future international order needs to take into account a number of unavoidable parameters, and that the UN SDGs represent a new approach to global politics in which these parameters are largely implicit:

1. unlike the previous Millennium Development Goals, the SDGs (while considering different national realities, capacities, and levels of development) are applicable to the whole world and not only to 'developing countries'
2. the 193 UN Member States are pledged to ensure that no one will be left behind and to endeavour to reach the furthest behind first
3. they presuppose the interconnectedness of problems and the need for a very broad agenda, integrating economic, social, and environmental dimensions; other global strategies are easily combined with the SDGs
4. the SDGs are action-oriented and look to a cultural change and to greater trust, as well as to material objectives

5. they seek to engage civil society as well as governments
6. they take as their starting point a shared and realistic understanding of the current global situation
7. they propose a timeline for the achievement of significant progress, running in the first instance to 2030

The SDGs embody, in embryo, a vision of the global citizenship of nation states and a common medium-term plan for humanity. However, the search for agreed criteria for action across political and cultural boundaries is very difficult given the complexity of the subject matter, the need to engage business and civic society, the breaking down of knowledge into specialised fields, new ways of manipulating public debate, and at least to some degree, a loss of trust in our shared future. It is difficult to leap over so many obstacles in one jump.

However, if we make the right intermediate moves in terms of orientation and methodology, we can help unlock the potential for a major future transformation at a global level. In systems biology, there is no privileged level of causation within a multi-level set of interactions (Noble, 2006). A piece of DNA, the environment, and a given phenotype are linked by means of biological networks that serve as pathways or filters. Life lies in the processes. In Chapter 3, we discussed the concept of 'positive peace' inspired by systems theory. Looking to systems biology for an analogy, we now focus on the processes that restrict harm and enable development.

If conducted under the broad conditions we describe below, the encounter between religion and human values, on the one hand, and global political realities, on the other, has transformative potential within a future life-giving multilateral diplomacy.

The hope that religious and secular leaders will work together and play their role in advancing civilisation is present in many religions and has been expressed with great clarity in the Baha'i Writings:

> Our hope is that the world's religious leaders and the world's rulers will unitedly arise for the reformation of this age and the rehabilitation of its fortunes. Let them, after meditating on its needs, take counsel together and, through anxious and full deliberation, administer to a diseased and sorely afflicted world the remedy it requires.

> (Bahá'u'lláh, 1973, p. 75)

Building new frameworks of engagement can prove decisive both for humanity in its present hour of need and for the future of religion and philosophy. To adapt Wittgenstein's image, neither religion nor philosophy should spin in a vacuum with gears that fail to engage the suffering of humankind.

International organisations, backed by governments, should use their convening power to initiate new, multilayered frameworks of engagement, bringing in the representatives of religion. Concepts having some of their roots in religion, such as mercy, patience, solidarity, reconciliation, grace ('a new beginning', the 'given-ness' of peace), and Gandhian satyagraha, as well as the axioms we are proposing in this book, can help us form a deeper understanding of how benign change happens. In support of new forms of consultation, the policy planning sections of foreign ministries can help develop new imaginative resources.

It is true that at the national and international levels, there are a number of existing channels for dialogue between government representatives and the religious communities. However, for the time being, this is a niche area: compartmentalised consultations lacking in political energy are not a likely pathway to a 'civilisational' transformation. It is appropriate, therefore, to explore in more depth how the active engagement of religious communities and others who adopt 'conscience-based' positions or 'life-stances' can contribute to peace building.

CRITERIA FOR THE ENGAGEMENT OF PUBLIC AUTHORITIES WITH RELIGIOUS ACTORS

As we signalled in the Introduction, there is a strong basis from which to start. Respecting the autonomous existence of religious or belief communities is accepted as an essential aspect of human rights protection. Equality legislation in several jurisdictions covers religious identity. Work has gone forward in recent decades to clarify the legal status of religious or belief communities and identify best practice or 'promising practices'. It is widely accepted that tolerance is an antidote to extremism.

The religious communities are recognised as having a role in the delivery of public goods such as education, healthcare, and integrating refugees.

Religious actors often play an important part in conflict resolution. Religions cross national frontiers. In the 21st century, can they help promote international reconciliation – as happened between France and Germany, and Poland and Germany, in the second half of the 20th century but conspicuously failed to happen during World War I?

There is a natural link between conflict resolution and strategies of prevention – such as educating for peace, and illuminating and motivating the broader politics of global peaceful transformation. We argue for a new sensitivity – a 'post-secular sensitivity' – to the role that religion can play in enlarging our understanding of the most pressing challenges of our time and unifying our efforts in response.

If our arguments are accepted, and governments begin to look to the religions for a contribution to a transformational multilateral diplomacy, what are the 'rules of engagement'?

This is an important question because, historically, cooperation between policy makers, other stakeholders, and religious actors has been a sensitive issue; misperceptions on both sides have created tension and alienation. The frameworks we establish should facilitate the effective engagement of public authorities with religious actors. At the same time, religious communities should act responsibly and with integrity in the public sphere. Satisfying these twin objectives will go a long way towards addressing the concerns raised by those who want to keep religions out of policy-making and the work of diplomacy.

Some of the specific questions that arise include:

1. What are the approaches, organisational principles, and values that allow the meaningful and effective engagement of policy makers and other stakeholders with religious actors?
2. Is the engagement with religious actors framed around specific concerns or conflicts, or is it a wider project, more a continuum than a series of events?
3. How can an organisation facilitating dialogue with religious communities and actors safeguard the distinctiveness of intergovernmental responsibilities, as compared to the standpoints and responsibilities of religious dialogue partners?

4. How do we ensure that a renewed attention to religion as a factor in global affairs and policy-making is oriented towards the dialogue around values, and does not focus on a religion or religions mainly when they are thought to be politically influential, economically strong, or numerically large and growing?

5. Should we try to ensure that the frameworks we establish are an opportunity for the religious traditions themselves to promote renewal – notably, through the greater involvement of women?

6. How can public authorities, while respecting the autonomy of religious communities, take into account their diversity and complexity, as well as the many institutions and associations that flourish under religious auspices? The religions could use the moment creatively in many other ways, for example, by starting new discussions or initiatives on issues of social justice, or by providing new roles for young people and the marginalised, who are often the most credible and effective communicators with their peers at the grassroots level.

7. Should inter-religious dialogue precede engagement with policy makers?

8. Are religious actors competent to negotiate on the main current challenges and, if not, how should they seek to communicate their religious perspective on specific diplomatic challenges?

9. Given that we cannot insist that policy makers engaging in dialogue endorse religion, or embrace the language and discourse of religion, how can we ensure that concepts and modes of action having their roots in religion are kept alive within the emerging culture and do not lose their meaning through secular 'translation'?

We believe that to address these questions will contribute to self-understanding on all sides and that answers will be found in a spirit of shared ambition and mutual hospitality. Once the modalities are clear, the detailed subject matter of the conversations that we have in mind will be determined ultimately by public authorities; this follows from the distinction, which we accept and value, between the secular and the religious.

It seems to us that, in principle, the invitation to religious communities to contribute to political deliberations should be open-ended within each national or regional context; inclusivity is an essential criterion. Perhaps submissions from interested religious communities should be sought initially in writing. Consultations with religious communities and actors will need to be extended through time and carefully guided. By a sifting process, the ideas that recur most consistently and persuasively, or seem the most likely to have an impact 'on the ground', can be used in formulating inter-governmental decisions.

The rules to ensure mutual respect, cooperation, and recognition between states and religious communities should always be compatible with broadening participation in a given framework to include other voices and stakeholders ('multi-stakeholder dialogue').

CRITERIA FOR NEW, MULTILAYERED NEGOTIATING PROCESSES

The new, multilayered negotiating processes that we have in mind should take shape in the light of a number of key requirements that are listed below.

GOVERNMENT 'INVESTMENT'

One of the main impediments to effective multilateralism, as the authors know from long experience, is that powerful governments do not always invest seriously in multilateral negotiations.

One good measure of the 'level of investment' is access by delegations to the decision-making levels in their home governments. In some international organisations, redundant, it is questionable how much time, effort, and 'political capital' are expended by prime ministers, foreign ministers, governments, and parliamentary committees on the objectives of a given negotiation. When a foreign minister attends a meeting, is it for the sake of that meeting or for wider networking purposes? Is the 'real business' being done elsewhere than in the multilateral forum in question?

When the management of a negotiating process is designed as a routine activity entrusted to mid-ranking diplomats, the inevitable tendency is to avoid innovation. The assumption is that the direction of policy has been settled; the role of diplomatic representatives is to project established 'values and interests', uphold alliances, and make space for the 'real negotiations' to go forward elsewhere, usually in very narrow circles. Secretaries of state and ministers do not want to be distracted from other agendas by new ideas 'affirmed from under' (as Seamus Heaney might put it) by delegates to multilateral conferences.

Another measure of commitment to any multilateral process is the allocation of resources, for example, to the budgets of international organisations, or to enable the recruitment of officials and experts to work in a particular area of policy.

A COMPREHENSIVE AGENDA

In view of the interconnectedness of issues and the need to bring emerging issues to attention, any new framework of engagement should have an open-ended comprehensive agenda, even if the 'sifting process' referred to above eventually leads to the setting of priorities. From the Conference on Security and Cooperation in Europe (CSCE),[2] we can borrow the concept of a wide agenda broken down into 'baskets' or dimensions. Balancing progress in one basket against progress in another is one of the arts of multilateralism.

A SLOW RHYTHM

A framework oriented towards clarifying shared values across several 'dimensions' needs to operate to a slow rhythm. The CSCE was conceived as a process and was conducted by means of a chain of conferences in several different capitals. Each conference was extended over years rather than months and included breaks for reflection and consultation. The United Nations Conference on Trade and Development (UNCTAD) has been gathering at ministerial level every four years for half a century or more; though it should be acknowledged that low levels of 'investment' by some players have prevented it from achieving its potential. The UN Law of the Sea Conference followed a similar, slow rhythm. If time is on their side, political leaders and public representatives can become accustomed, as they go along, to new ideas and build support for 'just transitions'.

'MULTIPOLARITY' AND 'TRANSVERSALITY'

Two common words in today's political discourse are 'multipolarity' and 'transversality'. By 'multipolarity' we mean the interaction and interdependence of many different actors. 'Transversality' suggests that actors in a particular category, such as governments, corporations, international institutions, NGOs, or religious confessions, do not talk only to their direct counterparts, but remain open to forms of dialogue that cut across categories and may prove transformative for themselves.

SUPPORT

A complex multilateral negotiation needs the support of disinterested officials who serve the process itself. At a minimum, logistical support is essential. In most cases, a secretariat or commission of some kind provides briefing material for delegations. Within the negotiations themselves, conference officers are needed – chairpersons of meetings, thematic coordinators, rapporteurs of meetings, and so on. As a delegate, a diplomat represents his or her government's point of view. As a chair, coordinator, or rapporteur, he or she is expected to act impartially in the role.

ACCESSIBILITY

There has long been a discussion within international organisations on how best to engage the media. As of now, very few multilateral negotiations are considered newsworthy from week to week or month to month. Interesting, informed, impartial reporting can help to make multilateral diplomacy accessible to the public, which under today's conditions is an important aspect of making it fit for purpose. Encouraging high-quality journalism will be an essential aspect of the multilateral initiatives we have in mind.

However, there is much more that can be done to promote 'accessibility' – by which we mean the awareness and engagement of a broad public. If the conference or process follows a slow rhythm, as recommended above, there may be scope to create consultative panels modelled on Ireland's citizens' assemblies. Under this model, an assembly or panel of individuals, including representatives of potentially disadvantaged groups, conducts hearings with a view to identifying possible 'landing places' for the formal negotiations.

The Irish charity First Fortnight creates a space in the cultural calendar where citizens can be inspired through arts and cultural events to talk about mental health issues in a non-scripted manner. The goal is to change people's perceptions about mental health. This can inspire change in public policy, public opinion, and within the creative arts themselves. The First Fortnight model could be adapted to the wider goals of a multilateral negotiating process.

A further option is to create a bespoke digital platform in support of any new process. International organisations already have websites and newsletters. There is scope to increase accessibility by the deployment of new digital tools. For example, 'quadratic voting' is designed to assess the priorities of a large number of individuals on a complex range of options. In the Colorado State legislature in 2019, more than 100 bills with a total price tag of $120 million were competing for funding of $40 million. Lawmakers were assigned tokens, which they could assign either in a concentrated manner to one or two bills or piecemeal to a broader range of bills. Two votes for the same bill cost four tokens, five votes 25 tokens, and so on ('prices' were squared, hence, 'quadratic voting'): prioritising a small number of bills reduced a lawmaker's influence across the whole package. Like the consensus-building citizens' assemblies in Ireland, or the proportional representation system used in Irish general elections, quadratic voting creates a different dynamic to decision making by simple majorities – and could be used for consultative or 'polling' purposes as well as for making decisions.

THE OUTCOME

In most cases, the structuring of negotiations implies in itself a broad outcome; so much so, that 'talks about talks' are often the most fruitful stage of any process to resolve differences by dialogue. A good example is the Northern Ireland peace process. The 'three-stranded' format of the negotiations anticipated the structure of the Good Friday Agreement (provisions regarding Northern Ireland, the island of Ireland, and the two islands).

In the present context, our orientation is towards a civilisational change, an Axial Age for an interdependent world. Our method is a multilayered negotiating process or processes designed to accommodate what really matters to human beings – conscience-based arguments arising out of religion, human values, life-stances, and philosophical first principles. In structuring a process based on such an orientation and such a methodology, it is essential to reflect in advance on the likely 'product'.

We suggest that any process of the kind we envisage should carry in its 'DNA' potential outcomes at three levels:

1. the gradual definition of new criteria or points of agreement (a 'matrix of principles') in the sphere of international relations
2. the progressive adoption of confidence-building measures
3. a paradigm change over time in our understanding of governance and of the economy

The classic example of a new 'matrix of principles' are the ten principles (the 'Decalogue') set out in the Helsinki Final Act of 1975. These principles established a political platform for an ambitious programme of cooperation.

We interpret 'confidence-building measures' in a broad sense to include new programmes and field missions at the international level, arms control measures, climate-related targets, measures to improve regional connectivity, joint initiatives in the sphere of education, joint humanitarian initiatives, the shared management of water resources; in fact, any measures with demonstrative value in the perspective of 'just transitions' and a future shared understanding of economic and political legitimacy at the global level.

The prospect of a paradigm change in our understanding of governance and of the economy is implicit throughout this book.

The diplomatic work we advocate will reflect a 'theory of change' in harmony with the SDGs but resting ultimately on an evolving cultural or 'anthropological' pattern. We seek a transformation at the level of habits and assumptions, a greater historical and religious literacy, and therefore also an enhanced capacity to work *systemically*, as our global situation requires.

CONTINUOUS REVIEW

We envisage a continuing process as opposed to a once-off negoti-ation. It follows that reviewing and refining agreed principles and confidence-building measures (CBMs) will be an important part of such an exercise as it goes forward. The review process should be understood as an extra dimension of the dialogue. Agreements may not need to be made legally binding or 'justiciable'.

In the Epilogue, a brief outline is offered of what an all-European initiative might look like if, in the early 2020s, there were the polit-ical will to inaugurate a European regional process reflecting the criteria set out in this chapter. In spanning cultural, religious, and political differences, an all-European conference could inspire par-allel initiatives in neighbouring regions: the Mediterranean, Africa, the Middle East, the Silk Road, East Asia.

NOTES

1 The Global Strategy can be viewed on the website of the EU External Action Service at www.eeas.europa.eu.
2 Subsequently, the Organisation for Security and Cooperation in Europe (OSCE).

REFERENCES

Bahá'u'lláh. (1973). *Tablets of Bahá'u'lláh Revealed after the Kitab-i-Aqdas*. Compiled by the Research Department of the Universal House of Justice, translated by H. Taherzadeh et al. Haifa: Bahá'í World Centre.

Francis. (2020). 'Letter to Popular Movements and Community Organizations,' Easter Sunday, 12 April. Vatican City: Libreria Editrice Vaticana.

Heaney, S. (1987). 'From the Canton of Expectation,' in *The Haw Lantern (Collection)*, p. 46. London: Faber and Faber.

Heaney, S. (1990). *The Cure at Troy: A Version of Sophocles's Philoctetes*. London: Faber and Faber.

Heaney, S. (1995). *Crediting Poetry: The Nobel Lecture 1995*. Oldcastle: The Gallery Press.

Lorca, F. (1960). 'Canción de jinete,' in J.M. Cohen (ed.), *The Penguin Book of Spanish Verse* (revised edition), p. 382. Harmondsworth: Penguin Books.

Mandelstam, O. (2008). 'Untitled Poem,' in Y.G. Fridstein (ed.), *Osip Mandelstam: What Agony! to Search for a Lost Word*. Moscow: Bagrius (bilingual edition of Mandelstam's selected poems).

Noble, D. (2006). *The Music of Life: Biology beyond the Genome*. Oxford: Oxford University Press.

Shelley, P. (2003). 'A Defence of Poetry,' in Z. Leader and M. O'Neill (eds.), *Percy Bysshe Shelley: The Major Works*, pp. 674–701. Oxford: Oxford University Press.

Varadkar, L. 2020. 'Leo Varadkar: "Thank you to the people of Europe".' *The Irish Times*, 31 January.

Von der Leyen, U. (2019). *A Union that Strives for More: My Agenda for Europe*. Political Guidelines for the Next European Commission 2019–2024. Brussels: European Commission.

Ward, G. (2020). 'Christian Hope Facing Secular Fatalism,' Loyola Institute Lecture, Trinity College Dublin, 31 January, 2020.

EPILOGUE
AN AGORA FOR EUROPE?

Philip McDonagh, Lucia Vázquez Mendoza, and John Neary

BUILDING ON EXISTING FOUNDATIONS

The purpose of this Epilogue is to illustrate our recommendations in a practical way – in particular, our recommendation that international organisations should use their convening power to bring about new, multilayered, consultative processes, inclusive of the representatives of religion, as an extra dimension within the wider project of making multilateral diplomacy fit for purpose. We offer a brief outline of what an all-European initiative might look like if, in the early 2020s, there were the political will to inaugurate a regional process of the kind we have in mind.

Our argument does not stand or fall by this one example – other formats, other pathways, other geographical regions may prove more relevant in the long run to the implementation of our ideas. In 2020, however, no region is better placed than Europe to promote the simultaneous objectives of (i) new forms of diplomatic engagement inspired by religion and human values; (ii) forms of outreach whereby a deliberative assembly meets a high standard of 'accessibility'; and (iii) a step change in region-to-region dialogue.

Post-World War II, Europe was at the heart of efforts to build global peace through solidarity. The EU, with its innovative economic foundations, remains the world's most important example of regional integration. The Council of Europe, which began its work in 1949, promotes a common culture in the sphere of human rights and the rule of law; this is understood as a continuing mission, underpinned by international agreements. The CSCE offered, in its day, yet another model of solidarity. States with different 'systems' acknowledged a responsibility, 'in the interest of mankind' (Helsinki Final Act, 1975[1]), to define common values and make shared commitments across a comprehensive agenda. One of the challenges facing Europe today is to continue to develop the EU without dividing the European continent between 'neighbours', potential 'neighbours', and 'non-neighbours' (cf. Francis, 2020), and without forgetting the UN and the wider interests of humanity.

We refer to the proposed Europe-wide conference or consultation as an 'agora'. In ancient Athens, the agora was the large public square and market at the heart of ordinary life in community. Though public buildings were found nearby, the agora was distinct from the assembly, the council, the law courts, the temples, and the theatre. The agora is where you would go to take the pulse of the people. Socrates spent his days there, in dialogue with all comers.

In 2012, Ireland, as Chair-in-Office of the OSCE, invested diplomatic capital in the initiative 'Helsinki plus 40'. The OSCE has a particular geographical scope; it includes the US, Canada, and the states of the former Soviet Union – the zone 'from Vancouver to Vladivostok' (as the phrase goes). The goal of Helsinki plus 40 was to revive the potential of the OSCE in time for the 40th anniversary of the Helsinki Final Act of 1975. This objective had the support of the EU. We looked forward at the time to building a 'security community' across the whole region – a zone of peace and active cooperation within which individual conflicts could be more easily resolved.

There is no space here to analyse the several factors that frustrated Helsinki plus 40 between its initiation in 2013 and its quiet demise in November 2015. However, it should be recorded, for present purposes, that during Helsinki plus 40 many governments were open to the idea of a summit, an all-European conference at the level of heads of state and government, provided it was well prepared.

In July 2017, UN Secretary General Guterres launched a Plan of Action for Religious Leaders and Actors, which includes the following proposal (p. 17):

> [The UN should] establish a world forum of religions and beliefs that would bring together an equal representation of religious leaders and actors, policy makers, educators, and media personnel from all world regions. The forum would deliberate on the role of religions in enhancing peaceful, inclusive, and just societies. The forum would have regional hubs.[2]

The 'Plan of Action', though not a document negotiated and agreed by governments, is an indication of the growing body of opinion supportive of international consultations in the sphere of values. We note that the Plan of Action envisages an initiative based on regional hubs.

THE EU CONFERENCE ON THE FUTURE OF EUROPE

As we write, in spring 2020, the member states of the EU, the European Commission, and the European Parliament are considering (under difficult circumstances) the convening of a 'Conference on the Future of Europe', to run to summer 2022. Much will depend on decisions taken under the German Presidency of the EU in the second half of 2020.

In its position papers and speeches, the Commission strongly emphasises the importance of giving citizens a stronger say in shaping policies. To this end, the Commission is open to new formats for consultation. It sees an opportunity to engage the support of the approximately one million persons who serve as elected representatives at different levels throughout the EU. The European Parliament has passed a resolution on the character and scope of the proposed conference. Organisationally, the Parliament's core objective is to involve citizens, youth, organised civil society, and a wide range of stakeholders in deliberations about the future.

All going well, the conference will build public understanding of the EU and its role in delivering objectives that the member states cannot deliver separately. To this end, the conference will consider both institutional questions and broader policy issues. The six 'political guidelines' or 'headline ambitions' for the EU proposed in 2019 by Commission President Ursula von der Leyen include 'a European Green Deal, an economy that works for people, and a Europe fit for the digital age' (von der Leyen, 2019). During the

COVID-19 crisis, public health policies and the associated budget-ary and financial issues have played a central part in the EU's delib-erations about the future.

GOING BEYOND THE EU CONFERENCE

It remains to be seen whether a process designed to consolidate the EU will have the time or the flexibility to look at global issues in the round. It seems to us that the construction of a common European home is more likely to flourish in the long run as part of a diplomatic step change at the global level. We have argued in this book that there is scope for a new 'Axial Age', in which the rules of society – at home and abroad – become more responsive to con-siderations of justice and are therefore more readily 'internalised'. There is an opportunity for the EU's Conference to do more than was originally intended; it can take an initial step towards a wider, longer-term, and potentially more innovative European consulta-tion with global resonance.

According to the Book of Genesis, God said to Abraham, 'Through you all the families of the earth will be blessed' (Genesis, 12:3). There is every reason to expect religious actors to support a new initiative oriented towards a deepening of shared values in an uncertain world. Rabbi Jonathan Sacks wants the Jewish people, with other believers, to be 'the voice of hope in the conversation of humanity' (Sacks, 2009, p. 231). According to former Archbishop of Canterbury Rowan Williams, the overarching issue of our era is 'how we keep alive a narrative about the interwoven character of human well-being' (Williams, 2019, p. 42). In his address to the Council of Europe in 2014, Pope Francis argues that tensions in Europe are 'sit-uated between multiple cultural, religious and political poles', and that we need a multilayered dialogue, or new 'agora', through which to build unity. In his speech on receiving the Charlemagne Prize in 2016, Pope Francis states that 'the soul of Europe is greater than the present borders of the union'. The Pope calls for 'the initiation of new social processes capable of engaging all individuals and groups' in the search for new approaches.

There is a potential convergence between, respectively, the unful-filled potential of the Atlantic, European, and Eurasian space, as repre-sented by OSCE; the UN Secretary General's interest in a values-led process to underpin and take further the SDGs; the EU's preparations for a conference on Europe; and the priorities of religious leaders.

DESIGNING AN AGORA FOR EUROPE

If our proposal for a Europe-wide initiative is to become a workable proposition, three principles need to be accepted:

1. regional and interregional cooperation is one of the new frontiers of diplomacy worldwide
2. in the global context, the post-war vision of a Europe at peace from the Urals to the Atlantic remains relevant; a 'European security community' offers a more meaningful point of comparison for Africa, the Middle East, or East Asia than the EU on its own, at least at this historical juncture
3. the rhetoric that equates 'Europe' and 'European Union' should give way to a practical proposition: *the continuing success of the European Union is an essential condition for a Europe at peace and for the progress of global diplomacy*

Russia, Turkey, and their European and Eurasian neighbours are likely to participate in a European regional initiative, for geographical, historical, economic, and cultural reasons. The presence of the US and Canada in any wider European process is desirable for historical reasons and because these countries are part of European culture in the broad sense. The UK would participate, as would Norway and Switzerland. The design of any multilateral process implies mutual recognition by the participants. Assuming that the three principles listed above are accepted on all sides, the EU will be well placed to play a leading role in shaping the new forum or 'agora'. The conference already planned for 2020–2022 could assume the valuable task of beginning policy preparations within the EU for the broader European process – which (for the sake of argument) could be endorsed at a Europe-wide summit in 2025, on the 50th anniversary of the Helsinki Final Act.

That we should use our resources and capacities to strengthen social cohesion is already one of the ideas underlying the EU's internal conference. Promoting, as well, a wider European conference, as a response to regional and global responsibilities, would be a valuable demonstration of the Union's capacity to act.

Our proposal is consonant with the vision of Robert Schuman:

> Europe will not be made all at once, or according to a single plan. It will be built through concrete achievements that first create a de facto solidarity.
> (Schuman Declaration of May 1950)[3]

A wider European conference, spanning cultural, religious, and political differences, can help inspire parallel initiatives in neighbouring regions: the Mediterranean, Africa, the Middle East, the Silk Road, and East Asia.

Broadly speaking, it would not be difficult to adapt the methodology of the former CSCE in order to 'image' a new, multilayered, all-European process. We think of such parameters as:

- serious political 'investment' in a new process, symbolised by a well-prepared all-European Summit, the first since 2010
- the primacy in any new process of government representatives, with decision making by intergovernmental consensus
- the choice of Europe as a regional hub within a potentially global project
- the concept of a wide agenda broken down into 'baskets'
- the rejection by participants of any threat of force with its corollary that the dialogue partners are equal
- the commitment to CBMs
- a sufficiently long time scale

In our vision, the process would involve the religious confessions, engage parliaments and civil society, and – taking societal differences into account – promote 'accessibility' along the lines discussed in Chapter 6.

The premise of the new agora or forum is that good conceptual work can help create an enabling environment for long-term evolutionary change without calling into question our ability to defend our immediate interests in day-to-day negotiations elsewhere. At a global level, two distinct and complementary agendas need to be advanced simultaneously:

- a long-term dialogue, underpinned by confidence-building measures, to ensure that the values that underpin diplomacy remain 'performative'
- day-to-day negotiations on the immediate issues

The all-European conference that we have in mind would address the first of these tasks. For member states of the EU, the second, more pressing agenda is suited to the conference that is currently being planned under the direct auspices of the EU. Our thesis is that a credible commitment to the first task gives us more 'breathing space' to address the second.

As well as the modalities for the all-European conference, the 'baskets' of issues to be examined within the new, long-term 'framework of engagement' should be defined, at least in broad terms, during preparatory talks. The structuring of future negotiations or consultations should carry in its DNA the probable results; so much so, that 'talks about talks' may turn out to be the most fruitful stage of the whole process.

SUBJECTS FOR DISCUSSION

Taking the CSCE process as a model, exploratory talks might work towards a future dialogue in five 'strands', covering, respectively, the principles of political legitimacy, three broad areas for enlarging cooperation ('baskets'), and the development of interregional partnerships.

In the first strand, under the heading of 'principles', participating states would reaffirm existing *principles* ('renew their marriage vows'), while addressing a number of issues on which there is as yet no clear, shared vision. How, for example, do we relate 'sovereign equality', as traditionally understood, to 'pooling sovereignty' within the EU, the 'citizenship obligations' of nation states, expressed, for example, in countless international treaties, and other institutional and regulatory realities?

In the *military/political basket*, participating states would need to revive an ambitious arms control agenda. Do we need, in addition, to set limits to espionage (a 'code of conduct'), especially in the light of growing cyber capabilities? Can we establish a metric measuring the arms trade against other security related expenditures, such as the budgets for multilateral diplomacy?

In the *economic and environmental basket*, learning the lessons of the pandemic, and advancing the SDGs and the UN's climate change agenda, would be central objectives. There would also be an opportunity to contribute to a global debate on the future of the economy and employment in the light of rising inequality, the impact of technology, the growing role of capital and finance (as opposed to income earned through work), debates around the fundamental purpose of limited companies, and of course the additional, even more radical, questions that flow from state intervention during the COVID-19 pandemic. Do we accept that markets need a political and economic context, including social solidarity, respect for the environment, and a culture of trust, that markets themselves are incapable of producing?

In the *sphere of human rights and humanitarian cooperation*, there may be scope for a 'whole-of-life' approach to human rights, as the EU's Fundamental Rights Agency has begun to argue. The process we have in mind would address the question of migration, either in this basket or – if demography and migration were to be treated as aspects of a single subject – as a separate work stream. The cultural impact of social media, guidance for the development of AI, and the regulation of the Internet are other potential themes for the third basket.

The fifth strand of our multilayered process would address a range of questions in the general area of *geographical scope* and *interregional cooperation*. By 'geographical scope' we mean the area of application of measures agreed within the process. This topic would lead naturally to the question of relations with neighbouring areas or counterpart organisations and processes: the Mediterranean, the Middle East, China, East Asia, the African Union, and of course the UN.

We have argued that any vacuum of values at the 'macro' level impacts on the prospects for peace in each individual context. A long-term, value-led, all-European political process can become the counterpart at a 'macro' level of continuing efforts to resolve individual conflicts within the region. Therefore, though we do not suggest incorporating existing peace processes or bilateral disputes into the proposed agora for Europe, a new all-European multilateral initiative, if it happens, will change the political context, create perspective, and bring a renewed sense of purpose to peacemaking at the subregional level.

A PATHWAY TO A BETTER FUTURE

The mark of personal and political maturity is that our most consequential responsibilities are acknowledged and addressed, not hidden behind specious rationalisations. It cannot be said that maturity has been the defining characteristic of multilateral diplomacy over recent decades. On the one hand, the SDGs represent, in embryo, a plan for humanity. On the other hand, the implementation of these goals is not proving to be a strategic issue for powerful governments. In channelling the work of international organisations into areas of specialisation and 'comparative advantage', governments have tended to shy away from the big picture.

That citizens have regard for one another, or nations trust one another, is not a 'constitutive choice' that we can make within the political process. However, actions of the right kind, even steps of a procedural character, can liberate a latent, evolutionary potential. By convening a new values-led process genuinely open to social transformation in the light of our deepest values, European governments can help us climb, as it were, to a higher pass in the mountains from which a better future as yet unseen can become visible for the first time. We must find the courage to believe, as Dietrich Bonhoeffer believed during the darkest days of the 20th century, that 'something new can be born that is not discernible in the alternatives of the present' (Bonhoeffer, 2017 [1942]).[4]

NOTES

1   The Helsinki Final Act can be found on the OSCE website at www.osce.org.
2   The Plan of Action can be consulted on the UN website at www.un.org. Its implementation falls under the remit of the UN Office on Genocide Prevention and the Responsibility to Protect.
3   The Schuman Declaration is available on the website of the Robert Schuman Foundation at www.robert-schuman.eu/en/declaration-of-9-may-1950.
4   See the early section of Bonhoeffer's letter under the heading: 'Without Ground under One's Feet'.

REFERENCES

Bonhoeffer, D. (2017) [1942]. 'After Ten Years,' in D. Bonhoeffer (ed.), *Letters and Papers from Prison*. Dietrich Bonhoeffer Works 8, pp. 37–52. Minneapolis: Fortress Press.

Francis. (2014). *Address to the Council of Europe*, 25 November, Strasbourg. w2.vatican.va/content/2014/november

Francis. (2016). *Conferral of the Charlemagne Prize/Address of His Holiness Pope Francis*, 6 May, Vatican. www.vatican.va/speeches/2016/may

Sacks, J. (2009). *Future Tense: A Vision for Jews and Judaism in the Global Culture.* London. Hodder and Stoughton.

Von der Leyen, U. (2019). *A Union that Strives for More: My Agenda for Europe.* Political Guidelines for the Next European Commission 2019–2024. Brussels: European Commission.

Williams, R. (2019). 'Strangers on the Shore,' *New Statesman*, 16–22 August, 2019.

INDEX